Non-Muslims in Muslim Majority Societies

CHURCH OF SWEDEN
Research Series

Göran Gunner, editor
Vulnerability, Churches, and HIV (2009)

Kajsa Ahlstrand and Göran Gunner, editors
Non-Muslims in Muslim Majority Societies (2009)

Non-Muslims in Muslim Majority Societies
With Focus on the Middle East and Pakistan

Edited by
KAJSA AHLSTRAND *and* GÖRAN GUNNER

☙PICKWICK *Publications* • Eugene, Oregon

NON-MUSLIMS IN MUSLIM MAJORITY SOCIETIES
With Focus on the Middle East and Pakistan

Church of Sweden, Research Series 2

Copyright © 2009 Trossamfundet Svenska kyrkan (Church of Sweden). All rights reserved. Except for brief quotations in critical publications or reviews, no part of this book may be reproduced in any manner without prior written permission from the publisher. Write: Permissions, Wipf and Stock, 199 W. 8th Ave., Suite 3, Eugene, OR 97401.

Pickwick Publications
A Division of Wipf and Stock Publishers
199 W. 8th Ave., Suite 3
Eugene, OR 97401

www.wipfandstock.com

ISBN 13: 978-1-60608-609-4

Manufactured in the U.S.A.

Contents

Contributors / vii

Introduction by Kajsa Ahlstrand *and* Göran Gunner / 1

1. The Status of Christians in the Islamic Worldview—*Mustafa Abu Sway* / 7

2. The Problem of Jurisdiction in the Contemporary Nation-State—*Jan Hjärpe* / 16

3. The Use of the Concept Minority: A Protection or a Burden in Relation to International Law—*Göran Gunner* / 28

4. Non-Muslim in Middle Eastern Muslim Societies—*Guirguis Ibrahim Saleh* / 40

5. Faith Based Organizations and the Configuration of Civil Society in the MENA-perspective—*Johan Gärde* / 51

6. The Status of Non-Muslims in a Palestinian State—*Bernard Sabella* / 73

7. Managing Christian-Muslim Relations in Pakistani Setting—*Mehboob Sada* / 93

8. Non-Muslim Women in Pakistan: Minority within Minority—*Yasmin Haider* / 108

9. Islamization of Laws in Pakistan and its Effect on Minorities—*M. Aslam Khaki* / 117

10. Non-Muslims in an Islamic State: A Case Study of Pakistan—*Ahmad Salim* / 133

Contents

11   Possible Strategies for Religious Communities under Threat—*Kajsa Ahlstrand* / 154

Bibliography / 161

Contributors

Dr. Mustafa Abu Sway is Professor of Philosophy and Islamic Studies at Al-Quds University, Palestine.

Dr. Kajsa Ahlstrand is Professor of Mission Studies at Uppsala University, Sweden.

Dr. Göran Gunner is Researcher at Church of Sweden Research Unit and Associate Professor at Uppsala University.

Dr. Johan Gärde is Coordinator of International Academic Affairs at the Institution for Social Work and Visiting Senior Research Fellow at the Department of Civil Society, Ersta Sköndal University College, Sweden.

Ms. Yasmin Haider, is Advocate at the Federal Shariat Court, Pakistan.

Dr. Jan Hjärpe is professor emeritus in Islamology at Lund University, Sweden.

Dr. M. Aslam Khaki is Advocate at the Supreme Court of Pakistan & Jurisconsultant at the Federal Shariat Court, Pakistan.

Dr. Bernard Sabella is a Palestinian Legislative Council Member and Associate Professor of Sociology at Bethlehem University (1981—1999), Palestine.

Mr. Mehboob Sada is Director of the Christian Study Centre in Rawalpindi, Pakistan.

Mr. Guirguis Ibrahim Saleh, is the General Secretary of the Middle East Council of Churches.

Contributors

Mr. Ahmad Salim is a poet, journalist, keeper of public records and researcher. He works at Sustainable Development Policy Institute (SDPI) as Senior Research Associate.

Introduction

Kajsa Ahlstrand and Göran Gunner

PEOPLE OF DIFFERENT RELIGIOUS belonging have in some geographical areas, as in the Middle East and the Indian subcontinent, lived side by side through the ages, sometimes in harmony and sometimes in dissonance. In other geographical regions, as in Scandinavia, societies have been religiously very homogeneous until recently being challenged by immigration. The implication is that the relationship between religious minority and majority is now on the agenda. The questions Europe and North America, with a Christian majority, and in Pakistan and the Middle East, with a Muslim majority, are now facing focus on the treatment and circumstances concerning minorities.

In order to discuss the situation for Non-Muslims in Muslim majority societies a consultation was convened with participants from Pakistan, Palestine, Lebanon and Sweden, both Muslims and Christians. Some work in academic settings, others in Faith based organizations, some in jurisprudence and others with theological issues. The papers presented at the consultation were "works in progress," and they remain tentative; the intention with this anthology is to provoker reflection and further thinking. Towards the end of the consultation, five distinct areas of concern were identified. The discussions were framed around power imbalances in relationships between powerful states/less powerful states and/or powerful religious communities and less powerful religious communities. Questions for further studies emerged, for example: in what ways is power situational? How does political power relate to economic, cultural, social, and moral power? What is the relationship between the local and the international? A religious community may be a vulnerable minority in a given place but belong to strong and numerous communities in an

Introduction

international perspective. Every religious community is a minority somewhere; some religious communities are also religious majorities elsewhere. The local/national majority religious community may perceive the local minority as a threatening representative of a powerful international community, whether it is "the powerful, colonial Christian world" of popular Muslim imagination or "the powerful, jihadist Muslim world" of popular Christian imagination. In both cases it is important to find ways to address fears so that the outcome may lead to peaceful coexistence between the communities. Some of the prerequisites for such harmonious relations are outlined in the papers presented here.

HUMAN RIGHTS

The fact that human rights are not divinely revealed but human constructions make them open to negotiation, interpretation, amendment, and discussion. They can only be implemented by humans, not by divine command. Although not instituted by God, the concept of human rights finds deep resonance in many religious traditions, including Islam and Christianity.

Human rights being human, they are thus inclusive of both women and men. In most cultures the specter of patriarchy—in the sense of a system that assigns subordinate positions to women in relation to men (including the kind of complementarity that assigns domestic tasks to women and social and political tasks to men)—is a case in point. Human rights are women's rights and women's rights are human rights.

Religious duties and rules must be seen in relation to human rights. There are cases when tensions between religious traditions and human rights run deep. Although there are no easy and universally applicable solutions the very fact that the tensions can be identified means that the discussion is not closed.

All member states of the United Nations are bound by international law, but there are violations of religious freedoms everywhere. To identify and make public such situations, especially when religious communities other than one's own are targeted, are important tasks for religious leaders in every society.

The definition of "minority" needs to be clarified. "Minority" in the Middle East often refers to the Islamic concept *Dhimmi*. *Dhimmi* (legally recognized non-Muslims in Muslim majority areas) were according to

Introduction

Shari'ah legislation protected by the majority but subject to special rules such as paying a poll tax and, in some cases, wearing of clothes that identified them as *Other*. When used in human rights discourse the term "minority" carries different connotations.

In democratic societies minorities have equal rights with the majority. According to international law religious minorities are recognized as minorities and should be granted rights of protection in society. A minority is defined as a group that in a given society has

- numerical inferiority
- social non-dominance
- sense of solidarity in the group
- shared history
- citizenship

THE VALUE OF A SECULAR STATE

These collected papers show that there are forms of secularism that are acceptable and even desirable for religious traditions. A secular state need not be regarded as inimical to religion; on the contrary separation between religion and state enables religious pluralism to be realized. Thus, it is desirable that the state is religiously neutral, treating different religious communities as contributors to the common good. The right to hold a belief and to pass it on to the next generation is central, as is the right to manifest one's belief in the public sphere.

There are different meanings of secularism/secular society. Some are ideologically opposed to religion and try to curb the influence of religion in all spheres. But there are also secular societies where people from different religious traditions are free to practice their religion in public. Religious people from different traditions may accept and support a secular society that is benevolent towards religion and appreciates the added values that religions might bring to their faithful: moral rectitude, responsibility in society, sense of direction, hope, and spiritual fulfillment. Religious people may thus support a secular state.

Introduction

THE ROLE OF EDUCATION ABOUT RIGHTS AND RELIGIONS

Some of the papers emphasize that in many parts of the world there is an immense difference between educated and uneducated people. The educated know about their own religious tradition, they are aware that there are variations within the tradition and they also know about other traditions. They know their rights—and they are aware of their responsibilities. This is not just a question of formal schooling; it is about attitudes to knowledge and formation. The kind of education which helps people to be proud of their own tradition but also to appreciate what is good in other traditions should be encouraged. This ideal is unfortunately often utopian, as many children do not even receive rudimentary education. It is, however, a priority not only to teach reading, writing and "catechesis", but also awareness of human rights and respectful knowledge about other religions.

IDENTITY ISSUES AND NARRATIVES

The question of education is closely linked to that of identity: how is "we" understood? Is the "we" defined over against/in contrast to "them"? Or can there be a "we" that affirms its identity together with the identities of other "we-s"? What narratives are transmitted from one generation to the next or from one group to another? In what ways can a group honor its martyrs and confessors without perpetuating inter-communal violence?

Emotion of belonging is a common human feature; to feel at home means that one is able to say: "we belong here." A national identity is often not sufficient; local identities may be more important. The problems arise when local identity groups vie for power and limited resources. Identity is not only a subjective feeling; it is often also a political instrument. Both religious and ethnic groups need to seek positive identifications that respect the dignity of other religious and ethnic groups.

INTER-RELIGIOUS DIALOGUE

The papers state two things about inter-religious dialogue: a) The alternative to dialogue—that is to isolate oneself within one's own religious community—is not a viable option; and b) Dialogue should be more about building trust and identifying common concerns than a conversation between doctrinal experts. During the consultation a story once

Introduction

told by Bishop Kenneth Fernando of Sri Lanka was referred to several times: "When my wife tells me that we need to talk I know that I am in trouble. But if she has made tea and we drink it together we also talk. This has taught me that it is better to invite our neighbors to tea than to dialogue." Some of the contributions emphasize that we are not just our religion; we are also professionals, citizens, human beings with physical, emotional, intellectual and spiritual needs. When inter-religious dialogue moves in the direction of inter-religious diapraxis (the practical reality of living and working together) it is more fruitful than when it is only about talking; while we strive towards common goals we also get to know and trust one another.

It is important that different Islamic movements (non-governmental institutions or independent scholars) are involved in dialogue/diapraxis, not only persons and organizations that have support from the state. Inter-religious relations differ from one area to another. Christians in Western Europe have different narratives of Christian-Muslim relations than those prevalent in the Middle East (where Christians tend to portray Muslims as Christian apostates or defectors). Some themes are identified as needing further elaboration:

- The image of the other in an inter faith-relationship
- The image of religious groups in the media and the responsibility of people involved in dialogue to oppose vilifications of religious groups in the media
- The other as a friend and as a threat
- Confronting stereotypes; religious Orientalism as well as religious Occidentalism

CO-OPERATION BEHIND THE BOOK

Behind this book stands a co-operation between the Christian Study Centre, Rawalpindi in Pakistan and several institutions in Sweden: the Swedish Pakistan Committee (Church of Sweden and Mission Covenant Church of Sweden), Studies of Mission at Uppsala University, Stockholm School of Theology, Church of Sweden Research Department, and Lund Missionary Society.

With these introductory remarks we invite you to read *Non-Muslims in Muslim Majority Societies*.

1

The Status of Christians in the Islamic Worldview

Mustafa Abu Sway

To understand the relationship between Islam and Christianity, and why Islam accommodates Christians despite serious theological differences, there is a need to explore the Qur'an and the Sunnah (i.e., whatever Prophet Muhammad, peace be upon him, has done, declared or approved as part of Islam), the primary two textual sources that form the Islamic worldview. It should be mentioned that in many theological and juridical cases the status of Christians is identical with that of the Jews.

Islam forms at once a continuum of the history of revelation and its culminating phase. Being the final revelation, it is entrusted with guarding the message of pure monotheism. This prototype religion that stresses the oneness of God was revealed to every single prophet or messenger. Despite unbridgeable post-revelational Jewish and Christian theological constructs, it is imperative for a Muslim to believe in their original revealed books [i.e., the Torah, the Zabur (Psalms) and the Injil (Gospel, in the singular)] and in their prophets including Moses and Jesus, peace be upon them. This is why Islamic theology and law (i.e., Shari'ah) accord a special status for Jews and Christians and refer to them in the Qur'an as "People of the Book."

In a tradition narrated in *Sahih Muslim*, Prophet Muhammad reflected on his relationship with the other prophets using inclusive language, saying:

> My likeness among the prophets is as a man who built a house skillfully and beautifully, yet he left one place without a brick in

one of the corners. People who saw [the house] were fascinated. Yet, they would exclaim why this brick is not in its place? He [the Prophet] said: I am that brick; I am the Seal of the Prophets.[1]

Islam also confirms the divine source of the *different* laws that were revealed to previous prophets and peoples:

> And We have revealed to you the Book with the truth, verifying what is before it of the Book and a guardian over it, therefore judge between them by what Allah has revealed, and do not follow their low desires [to turn away] from the truth that has come to you; for every one of you did We appoint a law and a way, and if Allah had pleased He would have made you [all] a single people, but that He might try you in what He gave you, therefore strive with one another to hasten to virtuous deeds; to Allah is your return, of all [of you], so He will let you know that in which you differed.[2]

There are ample verses and traditions that reflect the same inclusive and pluralistic ethos that was manifested historically at one point in the millet-system during the Ottoman Caliphate. This historical development permitted Jews and Christians to organize themselves and lead autonomous religious and communal life within the Islamic State. Today, Christians continue to have their own court system dealing with family laws in many parts of the Muslim world.

MARY AND JESUS

There are numerous chapters in the Qur'an that mention Jesus Christ's story including chapter 19 which is named after his mother Mary (Arabic, Maryam), peace be upon her. She is the only woman to be mentioned by name in the Qur'an, which shows that she is highly esteemed in the Islamic worldview as in the following verse:

> And when the angels said: O Mary! surely Allah has chosen you and purified you and chosen you above the women of the world.[3]

---

1. *Sahih Bukhari*, Vol 4, Book 56, #735 and *Sahih Muslim*, Book 30, #5673.
2. Qur'an, 5:48. M. H. Shakir's translation of the Holy Qur'an, published by Tahrike Tarsile Qur'an, Inc.
   It should be noted that traslations are considered interpretations of the Qur'an, which could only exist, qua Qur'an, in Arabic.
3. *Qur'an*, 3:42.

Jesus Christ himself is considered the word of God, to have performed miracles by leave of God and to have been rendered support by the spirit of the holy:

> We have made some of these messengers to excel the others among them are they to whom Allah spoke, and some of them He exalted by [many degrees of] rank; and We gave clear miracles to Jesus son of Mary, and strengthened him with the holy spirit. And if Allah had pleased, those after them would not have fought one with another after clear arguments had come to them, but they disagreed; so there were some of them who believed and others who denied; and if Allah had pleased they would not have fought one with another, but Allah brings about what He intends.[4]

In addition, the following verse reflects how the Qur'an describes the nature of the Gospel using beautiful words:

> And We caused Jesus son of Mary, to follow in their footsteps, confirming that which was [revealed] before him in the Torah, and We bestowed on him the Gospel wherein is guidance and a light, confirming that which was [revealed] before it in the Torah—a guidance and an admonition unto those who ward off [evil].[5]

There is tremendous love and respect for Mary and Jesus in the Islamic worldview and the hearts and minds of Muslims. This, however, is never translated into divinization, something the Qur'an repeatedly and completely rejects:

> And when Allah will say: O Jesus son of Mary! did you say to men, Take me and my mother for two gods besides Allah he will say: Glory be to Thee, it did not befit me that I should say what I had no right to (say); if I had said it, Thou wouldst indeed have known it; Thou knowest what is in my mind, and I do not know what is in Thy mind, surely Thou art the great Knower of the unseen things.[6]

NON-BELIEVERS

The Qur'an recognizes as true believers those who believe in the oneness of God, without associating anything or anyone with Him, for "there is

---

4. *Qur'an*, 2:253.
5. *Qur'an*, 5:46.
6. *Qur'an*, 5:116.

nothing whatever like unto Him."[7] None of His creation has divine nature. Therefore, angels and human beings, including all messengers, are devoid of any divine attributes. They are His servants, nothing more. The Qur'an responds to claims of Jesus' divinity, because he had no father, by reminding people of the example of Adam who neither had a father nor a mother, but yet without divinization. From a Qur'anic perspective, it is all about God's Omnipotence.

This is why in Islamic Shari'ah, despite the convivencia paradigm that Islam advocates in relation to the People of the Book, the Qur'an categorizes as disbelief several Christian theological constructs as in the following verses:

> They indeed have disbelieved who say: Lo! Allah is the Messiah, son of Mary. Say: Who then can do aught against Allah, if He had willed to destroy the Messiah son of Mary, and his mother and everyone on earth? Allah's is the Sovereignty of the heavens and the earth and all that is between them. He createth what He will. And Allah is Able to do all things.[8]

> Certainly they disbelieve who say: Surely Allah is the third [person] of the three; and there is no god but the one Allah, and if they desist not from what they say, a painful chastisement shall befall those among them who disbelieve.[9]

> And the Jews say: Uzair is the son of Allah; and the Christians say: The Messiah is the son of Allah; these are the words of their mouths; they imitate the saying of those who disbelieved before; may Allah destroy them; how they are turned away![10]

In contrast, the Qur'an praised those who followed Jesus Christ as a prophet:

> Then We caused Our messengers to follow in their footsteps; and We caused Jesus, son of Mary, to follow, and gave him the Gospel, and placed compassion and mercy in the hearts of those who followed him. But monasticism they invented—We ordained it not for them—only seeking Allah's pleasure, and they observed it not

---

7. *Qur'an*, 42:11.
8. *Qur'an*, 5:17.
9. *Qur'an*, 5:73.
10. *Qur'an*, 9:30.

with right observance. So We give those of them who believe their reward, and most of them are transgressors.[11]

This second group of Christians, compared in the Qur'an to Jews, is described as being closer to Muslims in friendship:

> (...) and you will certainly find the nearest in friendship to those who believe [to be] those who say: We are Christians; this is because there are priests and monks among them and because they do not behave proudly. And when they hear what has been revealed to the messenger (i.e., Muhammad) you will see their eyes overflowing with tears on account of the truth that they recognize; they say: Our Lord! we believe, so write us down with the witnesses [of truth].[12]

FREEDOM OF RELIGION

There are many verses in the Qur'an that advocate freedom of religion, without compromising truth or relativizing it:

> Let there be no compulsion in religion: Truth stands out clear from Error (...)[13]

> Say: [It is] the truth from the Lord of you (all). Then whosoever will, let him believe, and whosoever will, let him disbelieve (...)[14]

> And if your Lord had willed, surely all those who are in the earth would have believed, all of them; will you then force people till they become believers?[15]

> You shall have your religion and I shall have my religion.[16]

Coercion is absolutely prohibited. Islamophobic narratives attempt to portray the spread of Islam with the sword. The Shari'ah clearly prohibits forcing non-Muslims to become Muslims. Historically speaking, if Muslims converted others using force, there should be no Jews or

---

11. *Qur'an*, 57:27.
12. *Qur'an*, 5:82–83.
13. *Qur'an*, 2:256.
14. *Qur'an*, 18:29.
15. *Qur'an*, 10:99.
16. *Qur'an*, 109:6.

Christians in the Muslim world. Muslims had fourteen centuries at their hands to convert them by force, but they did not.

The memory of convivencia in Andalucia is well known and cherished. All three faiths were part of a thriving community. Christians and Jews took active roles in public life and their contribution to the Islamic civilization is well documented. In the eastern part of the Islamic state, Jews and Christians translated Greek philosophy and sciences. In both parts of the Islamic world, they became physicians, politicians and accomplished poets, to name a few achievements.

DIALOGUE

Another important argument against religious coercion is the existence of clear directions in the Qur'an to use the best possible methods of dialogue with non-Muslims. Why would the Qur'an bother about dialogue if coercion were an option?

> And do not dispute with the People of the Book except by what is best, except those of them who act unjustly, and say: We believe in that which has been revealed to us and revealed to you, and our Allah and your Allah is One, and to Him do we submit.[17]

Dialogue is seen today as an alternative to Samuel Huntington's 'Clash of Civilizations' theory. Inter-faith dialogue and the Alliance of Civilizations are only two ways that counter Huntington's theory which is based on what he perceived as conflicting cultural identities amongst existing civilizations. Economic injustices and ideological wars have no place in his theory! Islam does promote the idea that humanity has been created in different tribes and peoples so that they may know each other. The cultural differences such as different languages and "races," which the Qur'an refers to as colors, are celebrated as signs from God:

> And one of His signs is the creation of the heavens and the earth and the diversity of your tongues and colors; most surely there are signs in this for the learned.[18]

Of course, dialogue in itself remains elitist in terms of the participants, eclectic and reductionist in terms of the topics discussed, and sporadic,

17. Qur'an, 29:45.
18. Qur'an, 30:22.

for the high profile participants cannot commit themselves to prolonged periods of dialogue.

Apart from the naiveté associated with some participants' belief that they can change and fix the world in which they live, there is a need to address the real problems that plague the world today. Dialogue, when colonialism is still rampant and when the Security Council at the United Nations cannot stop the super power(s) from invading other countries, as in the case of Iraq, or allows the continued occupation in Palestine because of veto "rights," might be considered a pacifier, indeed patronizing, by those who suffer at the hands of occupiers.

The problem for some Muslims is that they consider the belligerent behavior of Western countries as a continuum of the medieval Crusades, especially when leaders such as President Bush use the word "Crusade" as part of their political narrative. This has negative implications for indigenous Christian communities in the Muslim world. It is morally wrong to blame our fellow citizens for policies of foreign countries. In fact, not all the citizens of these foreign countries support their governments, for we have seen demonstrations in many western capitals against the war on Iraq and in support of Palestinians.

THE STATUS OF BEING PROTECTED MINORITIES (I.E., DHIMMIS)

Since this section deals with the status of the Dhimmi in Islam, it is important to stress the Qur'anic dictum vis-à-vis human dignity in general before we delve into the verses and traditions that shaped the status of Dhimmis: members of the People of the Book and others (e.g. Zarathustrans) who enjoyed the same status by extension:

> And surely We have honored the children of Adam, and We carry them in the land and the sea, and We have given them of the good things, and We have made them to excel by an appropriate excellence over most of those whom We have created.[19]

When dealing with the notion of Dhimmitude, we face two types of generalizations. The first usually comes from Muslims who might not be aware of specific periods in Islamic history when Christians suffered at the hands of the official establishment. This was true during the reign of

---

19. *Qur'an*, 17:70.

the Fatimids in Egypt. The Fatimids were Isma'ili Shi'ites, and their rule was relatively short. It should be noted that the first victims of the Isma'ilis were the Sunnite Muslim scholars and political leaders.

The second generalization usually comes from Islamophobic institutions that make a living out of attacking Islam and Muslims. While whitewashing history is a vice, depicting all of it in negative terms is a clearly unjust position that does not recognize the tolerance that became a mark of Islamic history.

It is anachronistic to read the status of the People of the Book in ancient Islamic history in terms of modern notions of citizenship. Such Islamophobia never mentions the Prophetic traditions that deal with Dhimmis in general or Christians in particular. The Prophet hosted the delegation of the Christians of Najran at the Mosque of Medina for a few days. Muslims take pride in this story which continues to shape their religious character in relationship to Christians. There are many other traditions that deal with the Dhimmis using general language, yet reflecting the care and protection that Islam accorded to the non-Muslim minorities. In a tradition that was narrated by Al-Bukhari, the Prophet said: "He who kills a covenantor (e.g., dhimmi), he will be deprived of the smell of paradise..."[20] This hadith reflects the Prophet's message to his community that it is prohibited to harm a dhimmi, and that they will be held accountable on the Day of Judgment if they violate the Sunnah, which is binding to all Muslims.

THE PACT OF 'UMAR

The Pact of Umar Ibn Al-Khattab, the second Caliph, with Bishop Saphronious in 638 CE is considered the first post-revelational document to regulate the relationship between the ruling Muslims and the Christians of Jerusalem. It was an agreement to protect the churches and other important properties and rights. This agreement is celebrated by Palestinians and other Muslims and Christians. Nevertheless, Muslim scholars and intellectuals realize the changing times and, while they continue to be guided by the spirit of this pact, they subscribe to citizenship as a paradigm for coexistence.

---

20. Al-Bukhari, *Sahih*. Hadith #3166.

SOCIAL RELATIONS BETWEEN MUSLIMS AND CHRISTIANS

Muslims are allowed to eat at the table of the People of the Book, to trade with them and buy food, except for things such as alcohol and pork. Muslim men are further allowed to marry chaste women from amongst the People of the Book:

> This day [all] the good things are allowed to you; and the food of those who have been given the Book is lawful for you and your food is lawful for them; and the chaste from among the believing women and the chaste from among those who have been given the Book before you [are lawful for you]; when you have given them their dowries, taking [them] in marriage, not fornicating nor taking them for paramours in secret; and whoever denies faith, his work indeed is of no account, and in the hereafter he shall be one of the losers.[21]

This means that the maternal family of a Muslim could be Christian or Jewish. Beyond marriage, breastfeeding babies who are Muslims, Christians or Jews by the mother of one of the other faith, that makes the children all brothers and/or sisters in Islamic Shari'ah. Individuals in this relationship cannot marry each other when they grow up if they are of the opposite sex nor do they inherit each other.

Islam does not prevent Muslims from good neighborly behavior, or being good to one's family if they happen to be Christians or Jews:

> Allah does not forbid you respecting those who have not made war against you on account of [your] religion, and have not driven you forth from your homes, that you show them kindness and deal with them justly; surely Allah loves the doers of justice.[22]

---

21. Qur'an, 5:5.
22. Qur'an, 60:8.

2

The Problem of Jurisdiction in the Contemporary Nation-State

Jan Hjärpe

THE PROBLEM THAT I want to discuss in this chapter has nothing to do neither with the contents of legislation in any particular country nor with the actual rules to be found in any specific jurisprudence: either Islamic *fiqh* or Canon Law. The nature of the problem has to do with the question of jurisdiction. What individual or entity is regarded as having the right to decide? Who has (or takes) the right to decide what rule to apply, what interpretation to prefer, and to apply it in reality? The state? Some religious authority? The family or clan leaders? Some *vigilante* group? Or the conscience of the individual? Who is regarded as the legitimate judge or arbiter?[1]

In order to explain what I mean I will begin with a very special matter discussed very much in my youth, when I was still in school in the 1950s. At that time there was a hot debate in Sweden as to corporal punishment in the schools. The teachers still had jurisdiction. They could, if they regarded it as adequate, box a pupil's ears, pull a pupil's hair, or even beat a pupil. Spanking was regarded as an appropriate part of education. The teacher could decide to do it and immediately carry out the verdict his or herself. No legal proceedings and no trial were necessary. Teachers had jurisdiction themselves as teachers.

---

1. I have treated this question in the introductory part of a book on Islamic legal tradition, Jan Hjärpe, *Shari'a*, esp. 16–36.

The Problem of Jurisdiction in the Contemporary Nation-State

In the 1950s the discussion led to new legislation. The parliament instituted a law that entirely prohibited corporal punishments and chastisements in the schools, regardless of whether they were state or private schools. Thus, teachers lost their jurisdiction in this respect, even if they could apply other kinds of punishment.

The interesting thing, as I now see it, was that the debate had to do almost entirely with the role of corporal punishments: if they had a positive function or a negative effect only, if they were necessary for discipline in the schools, and if they were beneficial or harmful as a tool in the education. What was largely not seen during the debate was the interesting fact that this legislation was a part of a long process of change in the fields of jurisdiction. It was taken for granted during the debate that the state and its chosen parliament had the right to decide in this matter. This also meant that the teachers' right to spank the pupils could be seen as delegated by the state. In their capacity of being employed by the official sector of society they had a certain jurisdiction—not in any other capacity.

CUSTOMARY RULES, HABITS, AND LAW—A LONG PROCESS

The historian of law, Kjell Åke Modéer has studied the long and gradual development in which the courts of the state in Sweden were able to be accepted as having jurisdiction in more and more matters, for instance in fields where traditionally people in villages had applied their own customs or their own methods of arbitrating punishment for those who broke the customary rules and habits of the local community. The customary rules as to sexual behavior, betrothal and marriage were—with a certain success—superseded first by the rules of the church and then by the legislation of the state. The difference as to the content of these rules was perhaps not so great (at least not in the beginning) but the important change was that the idea of jurisdiction changed radically. The state's legislation was applied by the authorities of the state (and the church and the municipalities) and the function of the state courts was accepted by general opinion. The nation-state became the entity of jurisdiction. This meant that the local communities, the family, and other social entities had their jurisdictions diminished, often without being very much aware of this fact. The process coincided with the development of the nation-state (and later on the welfare state) as the main political and legal entity.[2]

2. Cf. Modéer, *Den svenska domarkulturen*.

So the state's legislation declared corporal punishments in schools illegal. A few years later the legislation was widened. A law declared it illegal for parents to spank their children. No corporal chastisement was permitted henceforward. This means that parents lost a part of their traditional right of jurisdiction. The state, and not the parents, had the right to decide. Again the debate was centered on the question of the actual function of punishments—were they good or bad? But more interesting, as I see it, is the change in jurisdiction: a wider role for the state and its authorities, a diminished jurisdiction for parents.

The changes in jurisdiction have to do with another phenomenon usually regarded as being connected with modernity.[3] Modernity is commonly characterized by a differentiation of both individual and societal functions. In the pre-modern society the roles and "identities" of the individual were intertwined. We can take as examples local communities anywhere in the world in ancient times, Northern Europe, Central Asia, the Indian subcontinent, Africa—wherever. It was taken for granted that most people would die within the same local community into which they were born. This was true also for a community of nomads—the circle of people which the individual was in contact with during his life was limited, and all his functions and roles had to do with little more than that specific group of people. This means that his life had a certain cognitive coherence. So much could be taken for granted. There was no doubt as to who should decide what. The individual, born within that village or group of people, had his "primary socialization" (i.e. learning to talk and understand, getting the norms of everyday life) and creation of his basic concepts and understanding of life in this limited circle, the extended family and the immediate neighborhood. If it was a man he would almost certainly marry a girl from the same village/circle and have the same kind of sustenance or profession as his father and grandfather.

Family and neighbourhood simultaneously constituted both the ritual-religious community and the circle of jurisdiction. The village council or family council had the customary right to decide and to judge in conflicts. The rites and rituals of the family, the village, the agricultural year, and the *rites of passage* of the different stages in life (birth and puberty rites, marriage, burial), were all intertwined. It had nothing to do with whether you were a believer or not—the rituals had their societal

3. Cf. Hjärpe, "Religious Affiliation," 119–28; Hjärpe, "Revolution in Religion," 111–20; Cf also Modéer, "Optimal Legal Cultures," 121–8.

meaning for the non-religious individual too. The religious narratives were integrated with the different functions of life, including the normative systems, and the distribution of "punishments" by the social pressure and the customs of the community. The village basically constituted a self reliant and endogamous community, whose "cognitive universe" for all practical purposes was within the frame and horizon of village life. "Custom" and "law" were more or less identical.

This characterization of a pre-modern local society is true for a village in old-time Sweden or for a village in the Subcontinent or Africa in ancient times. The long process of modernization (in its various stages) meant a radical change in respect to the individual's function and roles as well as his or her cognitive universe. Modernity includes a differentiation of these functions. Regardless of your background, regardless where you come from, it is very probable that you will die in another place than where you were born. Education today includes migration from the place of birth: schools, university, peregrination, studies in other countries. Knowledge, information and disinformation are transmitted by media through Cassettes, Video, DVD, TV, and Internet. Your profession will probably be different than your father's and grandfather's. Your marriage partner will probably not be a neighbor's daughter from your childhood and she will probably have a profession of her own. You will move in order to get jobs.

The professional community will be distinct from other groups of belonging, such as family, neighbors, religious community, ethnicity, nationality, or interest groups. But in all these different circles there will be a kind of jurisdiction functioning in different ways and in different fields of competence. The economic structure of family life is different from what it once was. A married woman will probably have her own income and contribute to the sustenance of the nuclear family, which will not be dependent on the extended family or clan—if the modern society and its conventional frame, i.e. the nation-state, is functioning adequately. The welfare state means that the traditional role of the extended family and clan has diminished. The traditional gender roles tend to lose their social relevance and to a considerable degree the same happens to other inherited normative hierarchies. They lose their character of being self evident. They are no longer taken for granted. This means that the traditional authorities are questioned. Who has the right to decide what is right and what is wrong? Who has—in reality—the authority to decide and the power to implement these decisions?

The differentiation comes to the individual's "cognitive universe" too. There will be a compartmentalization of how to understand and react to what happens in one's own life and in the world. The frame of the mental "system" is no longer life in a local community. You know, even in detail, events in other parts of the globe and what ideas are debated in other societies. Norms in this way become in a higher degree dependent on individual choices. The individual's social connections, their belonging to a professional community, a religious community or an ideological community, and different kinds of networks of common interest are not geographically limited.

GLOBALIZATION AND JURISDICTION

The nation-state, an idea that developed in Europe from the Westphalian peace negotiations in the first half of the seventeenth century became the form of societal organization in modernity. It constitutes the administrative framework possessing a high degree of compatibility with modernity, in relation to the technical development of new ways of communication and of industry superseding small village communities. Thus began the process of change in jurisdiction from the local to the larger entity. The state, in the word's modern sense, became the administrative entity encompassing smaller regions and their communities, but still smaller than a global political and administrational entity. The nation-state is something "in between" the local and the global. And here we can see one of the problems of jurisdiction. Who has the jurisdiction in the smaller local society, who in the nation-state, who on the global level? We have past from modernity to a global post-modernity.[4]

Our conference is a result of this development and it is the reason why we find it meaningful to discuss—in an international conference—Non-Muslims in Muslim societies. This is no longer a local question but is seen as globally problematic. By new communication techniques we can be in contact with colleagues, relatives, friends, people with the same hobbies (or ideas), or the same religious faith—or the same lack of religious faith—all over the world. (Do not forget atheists, those who deny any religious affiliation whatsoever! They do exist—I have met many from the

---

4. Cf. Modéer, "Global and National," 275–91.

Muslim world too. Likewise we should remember those believers who see their religiosity as a private matter and not as a legal affiliation.)

Even those who are small in numbers locally can constitute a distinct and even powerful community on a global level. One characteristic of this post-modern status is the availability of choice. We can choose among many competing ideas. The individual is aware of alternatives. The traditions, including the legal traditions and the hierarchies of norms have lost their self evidence. Religious affiliation can not be taken for granted. It is no more linked to profession, neighborhood, family or clan belonging to the same degree as it was before. This means that the religious community as a jurisdictional entity is more in question today than previously, as it is less linked to where you live, your profession, your interest groups, or your nationality (in the sense of citizenship in a state) than it has been previously.

Globalization means that the questioning of any legal system's relation to international declarations and conventions is inevitable. International declarations and conventions have a high reputation. To use their vocabulary and categorizations is almost a necessity, even when criticizing and refuting them. If a law system, a legal practice or legislation (of a state) should be founded on religious sources, as is the case in the Islamic legal tradition, some kind of at least verbal accommodation to these international documents must be developed. This is a fact. An early example of this is the Iranian Constitution of 1979.[5] The constitution declares itself as entirely an expression of Islamic law and Ja'fari jurisprudence, but its terminology and its structuring is very much in the model of other nation-state constitutions and of international conventions (not without influence from the earlier constitutional debates in Iran—especially the constitution of 1906).[6] This terminological and structural accommodation was a part of the strategy to get the constitution accepted, not only for an international audience but most of all for the reading audience in Iran itself.

It is necessary for leaders in any community, be it described as ethnic, religious, local, social-economic, professional or tribal etc., to stress *one* identity/belonging as the essential one in order to retain influence and mobilize support, and to minimize the role of all other identities, senses

---

5. Cf. Hjärpe, "Some problems," 52–69.

6. For the earlier constitutional development in Iran, see Hairi, *Shï'ïsm and Constitutionalism*.

of belonging and possible loyalties that individuals actually possess. An alternative strategy is to declare the different identities as interconnected. The religious affiliation is used for instance as a tribal, ethnic, national or social marker (a Muslim country, an Islamic state, a Muslim neighborhood, a Christian ethnic group, etc.).

THE EXAMPLE OF IRAQ

If we take the ongoing crisis in Iraq[7] as an example, we must ask the question in what respect Iraq can be said to exist as a state or as an entity of national identity. We can see that a kind of Iraqi nationalism and feeling of identity showed itself in late July 2007, when the Iraqi football team defeated Saudi Arabia, in the Asian championship. We could witness a national euphoria for a short time, a euphoria which certain groups tried to disturb in violent ways. What we saw in that situation was a battle over what identity should be regarded as the important one, a national identity or a specific communal one.

The problem is that citizenship in Iraq gives no benefits to the individual. The institutions of the state cannot be said to function in any sufficient way. Criminality is extremely common. No social welfare can be guaranteed by the state, no security, no participation in power, and so on. The nation-state is practically non-existent. This means that the individual by necessity is dependent on other belongings, other identities than Iraqi nationality. And this other network or "security institution" is almost always the extended family, the clan and the clan alliances, very often related to religious belongings (or ethnic, or professional ones, or combinations of all three). Such a network has its militia, its economy, and its representatives in the intricate political play in the country. It carries out its own verdicts, i.e. has its own jurisdiction totally independent of the state and the official administration which is too weak to impose any national legislation. The individual's loyalty to this network is then a pragmatic necessity. The different belongings in turn give rise to the possibilities of changing alliances. For instance, a Turkmen Shi'i group (most Turkmen are Sunnites) can get support from Turkey as they are "Turks" and from Basra as they are Shiites.

---

7. For the recent political development in the Muslim world, see Hjärpe, *Profetens mantel*, as for the situation in Iraq, esp. pages 106–41, Afghanistan, pages 65–84, and Somalia, pages 207–11.

The Problem of Jurisdiction in the Contemporary Nation-State

May I quote just one example only of this kind of web of "belongings"? In northern Iraq we find two Kurdish political parties, the KDP and the PUK. I doubt that we can find any difference in political (or religious) ideology between the two. But we know that the leader of KDP always belongs to the Barzani family and that the leader of PUK is always a Talabani. The parties can be described as clan alliances around these two families. We also notice that in the regions were KDP is predominant the Kurdish Kurmanji dialect is spoken and in the PUK region the Kurdish Sorani dialect. Then we can see that there is a connection between the Barzani family and the Naqshibandi Sufi Order. In the same way there are ties between the Talabani family and the Qadiri Sufi order. Both are networks existing in many regions of the world, even in Sweden. These different belongings can be actualized in various situations, such as in conflicts (or relations) with other ethnic groups in northern Iraq, the Turkmen and the Arabs. This is regardless of the formal religious affiliation (Kurds are mostly Shafi'i Sunni).

Likewise the groupings around various Shi'i religious leaders in Iraq, can be seen as a pragmatic necessity when the secular political, social and economic system is not functioning. This is also questioning the traditional role of the *marâji'*, the "sources of emulation," the old Shi'i religious authorities. But the main feature and characteristic, and the condition which creates this situation of competing jurisdictions, is the lack of functioning institutions in the state, its weakness and the lack of security. The *marja'iyya* is the tradition of family and clan relations to a *marja' at-taqlîd*, one or the other of the high Ayatullahs—now four of them are residing in Najaf in Iraq. Around them we can see institutionalized (and functioning) networks for mutual help and loyalties. We can see the connection between the Sadr family, the *Jaysh al-Mahdî* militia and the Da'wa party, the Hakim family and the Sciri party whose militia is called the Badr Brigades, and so on. Clan alliances and family relations are connected with whose jurisdiction one is actually following.

But this factor is of great relevance for the general conditions in the Muslim world today and so obviously for the immediate future too: the fact that the state and its institutions in so many countries and regions today are dysfunctional or even non-existent, as is the case for instance in Somalia, Uzbekistan, Afghanistan, Palestine, and to a considerable degree Pakistan as well.

THE EXAMPLE OF SOMALIA

Somalia is a strikingly evident example. It is a country whose borders are not defined, with a government unable to create law and order. There is a lack of any real executive power, the interim parliament can legislate but is unable to enforce or implement any of its laws, state institutions are none existent, the people experience a very insecure life and there is no functioning police or judiciary. This means that the individual is totally dependent, in order even to survive, on other networks, communities, and group belongings. What networks? Again we can see that it is the extended family, the clan, the ethnic subgroup (the tribe), the religious community, the professional community (the mafia, the tribal or group militia), or varying combinations of these. This kind of society is called a tribal one. Who in reality has any kind of executive power in Somalia?

The tribal war lords and the clan leaders possess this power because they have weapons and clan militias. Their will and whim have been so to speak the "law of the land"; a very detrimental situation for the people. Is there any alternative to the whims of the war lords? Yes, in the case of Somalia, we could see that people were becoming more and more interested in the so called Islamic courts and the idea of a divine Law, not dependent on the (non-functioning) legislation of the state. The idea of a divine Law, the Islamic Sharî'a, actually had relevance in the situation in Somalia (as elsewhere in situations where the state and its institutions are crumbling or lacking resources and legitimacy—such as in Palestine). However, the war lords have now come back, with the help of Ethiopian troops and support from the USA, and the Islamist groups have changed into guerrilla movements. The situation for the common people is now the same as before: insecure. Again we can see that the question of *who* has jurisdiction is in the centre of the problem.

GROUPS AND NETWORKS AND THE PROBLEM OF JURISDICTION

This tribalism is a consequence of the dysfunction of the state. A point here: for analyses and prognoses in the future we must consider that governments and state institutions are not the most important actors or agents in what happens. More important are networks not connected with states, citizenship, or governments. On one hand global networks of very different kinds are able to communicate on the Web; on the other hand

The Problem of Jurisdiction in the Contemporary Nation-State

weak governments, often without a popular mandate, and other institutions are unable to provide people with stability, safety, and welfare.

Let us consider the elections in Iraq in 2005. Between 100 and 200 parties (the number 191 had been mentioned in some research) were registered or attempted to register. Almost all of them were *clientage* parties, not ideological ones.[8] There were a small number of ideological parties, a communist party (mostly Shi'i), a liberal party, a social democrat party, and a handful of Islamist parties of various brands. But these groups won very few seats in the parliament. The voters cast their votes for traditional "security systems," that is parties connected with ethnic groups, religious communities, or clan alliances. Of the 275 seats in the parliament, only about 10 went to parties that can be called ideological. I want to stress this point: the parties were connected with family alliances. In some cases the religious affiliation is a marker of clan belonging, but the main definition of belonging was in reality the family affiliation. This will probably continue in the future. Who dares to trust the state under present conditions? Tribalism will prevail for a considerable time.

Let us for a moment consider the recent events in Pakistan, centered in and around the Lal Mosque in Islamabad during the month of July 2007 in relation to the problem of jurisdiction. As we know, the groups in and around the Lal Mosque aspired just to that, to have jurisdiction. A special "Islamic court" was installed in the Mosque and challenged the official judiciary of the state. Vigilante groups put their interpretation of Sharî'a rules into praxis attacking shops, and night clubs, and amusement centers of different kind, imposing by force (but without sanction from the state) their idea of an Islamic order in society. This is a challenge not only to the state but also a challenge for the traditional religious authority. Simultaneously the legal legitimacy of the Musharraf regime is challenged by the state judiciary and the (secular) legal authority—the conflict between Musharraf and Iftikhar Mohammad Chaudhry. Who represents the legal authority, who has the right of jurisdiction, and jurisdiction over whom? What is the relation between citizenship and legal belonging? What is—in reality—the relation between the conditions due to citizenship and the conditions due to *other* belongings, kinship, social,

---

8. As for the concept of clientage parties, see the PhD thesis by Ann-Kristin Jonasson, *At the Command*. She analyses in her thesis the actual function of three parties, the Fazilet Partisi in Turkey, the Jabhat al-'Amal al-Islâmîin Jordan and the Jamaat-i Islami in Pakistan.

religious, ethnic, or professional identity? Who is the judge in the various fields of legality (criminal law, economic rules, personal law [*akhwâl shakhsiyya*])?

As for vigilante groups, we can compare this with the mutawi'ûn in Saudi Arabia (*hay'at al-amr bi l-ma'rûf wa n-nahy 'an al-munkar*), the semi-official "religious police," just now in a conflict of jurisdiction with the legal authorities.[9] Similar, but less officially recognized groups can be found in other regions too.

May I mention that I have had some interest in the function of personal law in Syria? As we know the legislation demands that marriages are registered at the state/municipal administration. But I would say that only a minority of marriages are registered in those official archives. As a rule people in general regard the Nikah contract written by the families to be enough. The families thus regard themselves as having the jurisdiction in family matters, not the state.

CHANGE IN RELIGIOUS AUTHORITY

My last point has to do with the change in religious authority. Religious leaders, in the meaning of those in leading positions in traditional religious institutions, such as popes, patriarchs, grand muftis, community leaders and so on, have lost both power and influence. This is due to several factors, among them the development of media, the rapid changes in social structures, the globalization, and actual secularization (which I have noted is on the increase during recent years). This means that traditional religious leaders are in reality not very representative for their communities and their pronouncements are not reflecting what people in general think and how they act. There are a multitude of others who claim jurisdiction, with or without religious vocabulary. That is a fact. Young people meet this on the Web, and they very much take part in the debate there. Take a look at the Internet cafés in Iran or Egypt. They are jammed with young people engaged in the immense global flow of information, disinformation, propaganda, discussions, even Web wars. You can find everything there, from extreme jihadism, and recruitment pages for being a volunteer in Chechnya, to the most liberal, modernist, democratic Islamism, from Deobandi Taliban traditionalism to the mildest introvert Sufism. The young individual can choose, no, they have to choose. A per-

---

9. Cf. MacLeod "Vice Squad," 33–35.

son can one day accept one standpoint and another day the opposite. We can see very fast processes of change. The individual oscillates between different belongings or "identities."

We must consider that specific religious affiliation is *not* a determining factor. There are more belongings to take into account. The *roles* of religious belonging change as the political conditions change, the strength or weakness of the state being one of the most important factors. A very strong state in the sense of a nation-state having the actual power to impose its legislation in reality is something quite different from a weak one, where the state jurisdiction is very much challenged and in reality supplanted by others having or claiming jurisdiction—among them leaders of religious communities, groups, or cults (i.e. *ad hoc* movements). And the authority of religious leaders—is it seen as a delegation of the state, or due to something else? In our conference the focus is on Pakistan and the Middle East. In both regions states are weak in this sense. So who are those claiming jurisdiction and what are people's responses to their different claims? The conditions are not something constant, unchangeable. And the actual function of religious affiliation is changing due to new conditions. We can not regard traditional religious leaders as given representatives of their communities. Their utterances have a low prognostic value as, as we can see, people do not act according to them.

What is the actual role of the different belongings of the individual? What is the function of citizenship in relation to the other collective identities of the individual locally or on the global level? What is the jurisdiction of the professional community, kinship, and the religious community? As for religious rules: *who* decides (in reality) their application for the individual? Is it the state and its judiciary; the religious community leaders; vigilante groups; or the individual's own conscience? Are religious rules laws or are they admonitions, moral advice? And what to do with the increasing number of explicit non-believers or those who do not regard affiliation to a specific religious community as an essential part of their identity, preferring to identify oneself with nationality, ethnicity, profession, or perhaps political ideology?

3

The Use of the Concept Minority

A Protection or a Burden in Relation to International Law

Göran Gunner

MY POINT OF DEPARTURE is an assumption that the member-states of the United Nations are legally and morally bound by international laws, but at the same time violations against human rights, and not the least freedom of religion, are taking part all over the world. Violations against freedom of religion may be experienced by Muslims and Muslim communities in Sweden as well as in other Western European countries. The reality for Christian individuals and Christian communities, as minorities in Pakistan and in countries in the Middle East, is the same. Even if I know that the use of the concept "minority" is "a hot issue" not the least in the countries of the Middle East, I will address the concept since it is included in the regulations of international law.

BELONGING AND RELIGIOUS COMMUNITIES IN THE MIDDLE EAST

A hollow clattering sound is reaching the nearest neighborhood with stubborn regularity. It is the monastery calling for The Divine Liturgy. A small piece of wood suspended with two chains immediately outside the door of the church in the monastery is used as the church bell. Some of the monasteries in the Middle East have kept an old tradition from Ottoman time when they were forbidden to use church bells made of iron. Instead they banged on wood telling the faithful Christians about the time of service. You may see and hear it at St. James in the Armenian Quarter in Jerusalem. Today a piece of wood is a reminder of times with strict rules concerning the Christian community, or if you want a minority, living in a Muslim majority society. This is just one example of the historic shadow still present among Christian communities in the Middle East.

Today, Christian communities are scattered among a number of states in the Middle East but are still living with a long tradition and history in the region. In Iraq Christians can, in the modern terminology, claim that the patriarch Abraham was an Iraqi from Ur in Chaldea. In Egypt the Copts claim to be the offspring of the pharaohs, the Maronites of Lebanon talk about the Phoenicians as a historic starting point, and in Jerusalem they talk about the birth of the early church. Archaeological evidences point to a widely spread Christian culture from the fourth century and onward. This helps to legitimize a presence, long historic continuity, and genuine belonging. The presence is often described as being indigenous including claims of historical presence in the region predating the spread of Islam. Of course, the Christian presence has never been isolated but through the centuries in a high degree contributing to the cultural, social, economical, and political development of the region. At the end of the nineteenth century it became common among Christians to talk about *watan,* the homeland with definitions of citizenship and judicial systems based on non-religious and secular principles. To religious communities it would imply a society looking upon everybody as equal citizens in the state.

The feeling of belonging has during the last twenty years been put into print through Christian authors and priests living in Israel and Palestine. The book of father Elias Chacour introduce the belonging already in the title, *We belong to the land.*[1] Elias Chacour, Audeh Rantisi,[2] Naim Ateek,[3] and Mitri Raheb[4] have all been influenced by the occurrences in Palestine 1947–1948. All of them describe the banishing of the Palestinians, Christians as well as Muslims, being forced to leave the land they had belonged to since generations. They all talk about the importance of a piece of land where to live and work. Naim Ateek inspired by Latin American liberation theology develops a Palestinian theology of libera-

1. Chacour, *We belong.*
2. Rantisi, *Blessed are the Peacemakers.*
3. Ateek, *Justice, and Only Justice.*
4. Raheb, *I Am a Palestinian.*

tion. The historian Albert Aghazarian has reflected on the importance of looking upon the own roots integrated in the Arabic-Islamic heritage and the culture of the Mediterranean as well as a universal approach.[5] In stressing this identity the focus is on a joined present situation and a future for all citizens in one and the same national unity. The specific Christian heritage does not disappear but there is a strong opposition against being called minority and the Christians want to be considered as parts and parcels of national identity.

The Coptic pope Shenouda III opposed officially 1994 the use of the concept minority as a description of the Coptic citizens of Egypt. The background was the joint venture by the organization Ibn Khaldoun Center in Cairo and the Minority Rights Group in London to conduct a conference in Cairo under the title: "The United Nations Declaration on the Rights of Minorities and Peoples in the Arab World and the Middle East."[6] A storm of protests, not least in media, opposed the idea of the Copts as a minority and instead they emphasized the Coptic belonging to Egypt and the concept of citizenship. It was in relation to this conference the Pope expressed the opinion that the idea of making any division out of majority—minority perspective was discriminating, separating, and distinguishing. According to the Pope, the Copts do not want to call themselves minority neither do they want others to do so.[7] The discrepancy was obvious between those claiming the Cops not to be a minority but an integral part of the very complex Egyptian society and those who claimed that the problems of the Copts as a religious minority do exist and are in need of being taken seriously.

A tension appears between the traditional meaning of minority in the Middle East with clear references to the millet-system and the use of minority in the international human rights system. Communities in the Middle East obviously defend themselves against ideas possible to interpret as a return to or any effort of establishing any system treating them as second class citizens. Instead they claim equality and to be equal citizens.

---

5. Sabella et al. *On the Eve*.

6. "The Conference on the United Nations Declaration on the Rights of Minorities and Peoples in the Arab World and the Middle East." A report was published before the conference: Ibrahim, *The Copts of Egypt*.

7. "Egypt: Violations."

The Use of the Concept Minority

BELONGING AND MINORITIES IN PAKISTAN

It is rather crowded with people in some of the suburbs of Lahore and you may even call Shah Dara Koi a slum district. On Sundays the faithful occupy every single spot in the church and when the service starts it goes out in the surrounding area through a loud-speaker at the top of the church building, even to the Muslim neighbors. And one of the church-leaders explains it with; of course:

> We are part of this area, we belong, and even if we are part and parcel of the Christian minority we are Pakistanis.

It is interesting to see that, when the Christian Study Centre in Rawalpindi offers an extensive program on "Interfaith, Ecumenical, cross-cultural Study and Exposure Program" in Pakistan, the lecturers very much describe the Christian position out of a minority perspective. It is about "Dialogue from a minority perspective." It is about "Religious Minorities in Pakistan: Struggle for Identity," and about "Islamization and its effects on Minorities." The same is reflected in the publications from the Christian Study Centre[8] as well as in the life of the Pakistani Churches, both Protestant and Catholic. The National Commission for Justice and Peace of Pakistan connected to the Catholic Bishops' Conference of Pakistan has published extensive reports on the religious minorities in Pakistan.[9] The commission has also presented their case to the UN Commission on Human Rights Working Group on Minorities as a minority case. I quote:

> Theoretically the Constitution of Pakistan provides religious freedom and safeguards to religious minorities. However continued incidents of violence against religious minority groups, attacks and destruction of their places of worship, killing and rape of the members of minority communities, is a matter of grave concern.[10]

The Christian community in Pakistan is rather outspoken about violations of human rights directed against them because of their religious belonging.

The important focus in the Middle Eastern countries as well as in Pakistan is on a common national identity with citizenship and solidar-

---

8. Moghal and Jivan, *Religious minorities*. See also articles published in *al-Mushīr*, published by the Christian Study Centre, Rawalpindi.

9. See for examples: "A Report on," 2004; 2007.

10. "Agenda Item: 3 (a)."

ity with the country as the basic originator of identity. At the same time, in the Middle East the emphasis has been put on belonging to the national identity and in Pakistan there is an emphasis on being a religious minority.

In the academic literature the concept of minority is frequently used in relation to the Middle East as *Minorities and the State in the Arab World*, *Middle Eastern Minorities and Diasporas* and *Religious Minorities, Nation States and Security* and in relation to Pakistan as *Religious minorities in Pakistan: struggle for identity* and *Religious minorities in Pakistan*.[11]

RELIGIOUS DIVERSITY

In societies with religious diversity, as well as in all societies there is a need for freedom of religion and belief, freedoms that may be restricted in a democratic society but should be protected by legal obligations.

Jenny E. Goldschmidt and Titia Loenen discuss in an article the position of the State in a religiously pluralist society and look into preconditions for guaranteeing freedom of religion and belief.[12]

The first precondition is the separation of state and religion; in the European case usually between church and state. Of course, different national systems will have different concepts of secularity but there need to be constitutional protection enabling pluralism to be realized. A second precondition closely connected to the first can be the neutrality of the state even if the state seems to take into account values reflecting a dominant culture. I am aware there are plenty of definitions and interpretations of both secularity and neutrality but what I aim at is a model that offers a framework for an implementation of human rights to all. This includes both openness to 'others' in the society as well as a freedom of choice to belong to a particular group or not.

The rights must include both the *forum internum*, the right to hold an inner belief or you may say a conviction by heart, and the *forum externum*, the right to manifest the belief in public as well as privately. Freedom of religion is not to be spared from religious symbols in the public space or to prohibit religious manifestations so that people should be exempted from any public expression of religious activities. Important to the reli-

---

11. Ma'os, and Sheffer, *Middle Eastern Minorities*; Apostolov, *Religious Minorities*; Bengion, and Ben-Dor, *Minorities and the State*.

12. Goldschmidt and Loenen, "Religious Pluralism."

gious communities and a prerequisite for a sustainable democratic society is the protection of the right to religious freedom and freedom of belief (civil and political), the protection of freedom of assembling, freedom of expression, freedom of choice for the individual, and a fair and equal treatment by the state of all religious communities. That would accommodate a diversity of religious communities. And it may be possible due to national law and national implementation of the international conventions and applicable declarations.

To follow the religious rules is necessary for a pious individual living the everyday life without ending up in conflict with the prescriptions of religion and the conscience. But the interpretation made by the authorities and the needs of a religious community are not always talking the same language. Of course, it is the normative way of interpreting the existing laws that counts. That the reality of freedom of religion would be questioned by religious communities as well as by individuals seems to be a surprise or looked upon with ignorance by the authorities. The concept of religion used by the state and the daily experience by religious persons is not the same and the problem becomes obvious when the authorities seem not to care. This leaves us with the important and unsolved question: What is the meaning of religious freedom in the society? It is important that freedom of religion is not restricted to the mind and the religious ideas but also include rituals and religious action. Freedom of religion and freedom of choice for the individual are important values.

Religious people usually do not live in isolated sectors of the society but are involved in everyday life as citizens and as belonging to the society. A usually dominant position by majority religious groups is at the same time usually in a high degree influencing the public and the private spheres in society. Some would claim that historical, social-demographical and religious factors make that kind of dominant positions unavoidable.[13] But it raises questions: How to deal with religious diversity? And how to deal with not being violated against due to religious belonging? How to be able to practice one's religiosity individually and as a religious community? In relation to international law and human rights issues it seems to be two different options. Either you emphasize being equal nationals in a democratic society or you emphasize being a religious minority in a religious majority society.

---

13. Bijsterveld, "Equal Treatment."

EQUAL NATIONALS IN A DEMOCRATIC SOCIETY

Human rights, or if you want to use the concept human dignity, is protected by several UN declarations and covenants. A good point of departure is *Article 2* in the Universal Declaration of Human Rights which includes non-discrimination:

> Everyone is entitled to all the rights and freedoms set forth in this Declaration, without distinctions of any kind, such as race, colour, sex, language, religion, political or other opinion, national or social origin, property, birth or other status.[14]

This principle of non-discrimination is then anchored in the international law with the intention of being a guiding principle for national law and working through implementation at all levels in the societies. There are two types of equality provisions. The States are obliged to guarantee the treaty's rights to all individuals under their jurisdiction. The other prohibit discrimination reaching further than the rights in the treaties themselves with equality of opportunities, equality before the law, and protection from discrimination in any context.[15] These latter do not impose on a specific State to undertake measures. Of course, that is a problem. You may, as belonging to a specific religious community, have all the protection you need in for example a Constitution but the State is not obliged to do any affirmative action to upgrade the rights for what is considered to be a "foreign" belief in a dominant society. And when a specific State does not guarantee or protect the direct provisions in the treaties there is an obvious problem for the individuals belonging to a religiously different community than the dominant one.

But the international law is clear about religious freedom as is demonstrated in the International Covenant on Civil and Political Rights stating in *Article 18*:

> 1. Everyone shall have the right to freedom of thought, conscience and religion. This right shall include freedom to have or to adopt a religion or belief of his choice, and freedom, either individually or in community with others and in public or private, to manifest his religion or belief in worship, observance, practice and teaching.

---

14. *Universal Declaration.*
15. Fottrell, "Ever Decreasing Circles."

The Use of the Concept Minority

2. No one shall be subject to coercion which would impair his freedom to have or to adopt a religion or belief of his choice.

3. Freedom to manifest one's religion or belief may be subject only to such limitations as are prescribed by law and are necessary to protect public safety, order, health, or morals or the fundamental rights and freedoms of others.

4. The State Parties to the present Covenant undertake to have respect for the liberty of parents and, when applicable, legal guardians to ensure the religious and moral education of their children in conformity with their own convictions.

The covenant talks about both religion and belief of choice, the right to manifest religion or belief and not allowing coercion. The UN-system issues General Comments with normative interpretation of the covenant. In General Comment number 22 it is explained:

> Article 18 protects theistic, non-theistic and atheistic beliefs, as well as the right not to profess any religion or belief. The terms "belief" and "religion" are to be broadly construed. Article 18 is not limited in its application to traditional religions or to religions and beliefs with institutional characteristics or practices analogous to those of traditional religions. The Committee therefore views with concern any tendency to discriminate against any religion or belief for any reason, including the fact that they are newly established, or represent religious minorities that may be the subject of hostility on the part of a predominant religious community.

The comment also gives examples of what is considered to be under protection:

1. Ritual and ceremonial acts giving direct expression to belief;
2. The building of places of worship;
3. The use of ritual formulae and objects;
4. The display of symbols;
5. The observance of holidays and days of rest;
6. The observance of dietary regulations;
7. The wearing of distinctive clothing or head coverings;
8. The use of a particular language customarily spoken by a group;

9. The freedom to prepare and distribute religious texts or publications.

Of course, it is possible to continue quoting declarations and covenants but this may be enough to claim there is a protection for religious people and communities in the combination of equal human rights for everyone and the freedom of religion and belief. May be, that is the way chosen by the communities in the Middle East claiming belonging.

RELIGIOUS MINORITIES IN A RELIGIOUS MAJORITY SOCIETY

Against the relief of a dominant society or a majority culture completely ignoring or even opposing giving space for people of other faith and thereby not giving equal possibilities for other religious expressions than the dominant, you need to further on into the international law.

That will open up talk about non-Christian religious communities in Europe and non-Muslim religious communities in Muslim countries. The abuse hurts the individual but it also hurts all individuals as part of a community. The international law will then offer the possibility to use the concept of minority.

In an article about construction and contingency of the minority concept Eric Heinze explains:

> Minority status thus comports its own spectrum of norms. At one extreme would be integrationist non-discrimination rights; at the other, non-assimilationist group rights. Between the two, various blends are possible, according to the specific circumstances and aspirations of each group or of its members.[16]

A critical issue is the increase of national minorities with ethnic and linguistic aspirations claiming their rights. But for many religious groups in Pakistan and in the Middle East there are no national aspirations since they are not foremost national, ethnic or linguistic but religious communities and part of the national and linguistic surrounding society. The lack of national aspirations would sometimes be questioned by parts of the community immigrating to the Diaspora in America or Western Europe.

Group rights or minority rights as such are under question even in the human rights discourse but the rights concerned can be looked upon

16. Heinze, "The Construction."

as rights of individuals as members of their group. It is about the rights of the individual as belonging to a group. *Article 27* of the International Covenant on Civil and Political Rights (ICCPR) states:

> In those States in which ethnic, religious or linguistic minorities exist, persons belonging to such minorities shall not be denied the right, in community with the other members of their group, to enjoy their own culture, to profess and practice their own religion, or to use their own language.

In a General Comment number 23 given to article 27 it is emphasized that no one are excluded:

> Article 27 confers rights on persons belonging to minorities which "exist" in State party. Given the nature and scope of the rights envisaged under that article, it is not relevant to determine the degree of permanence that the term "exist" connotes. Those rights simply are that individuals belonging to those minorities should not be denied the right, in community with members of their group, to enjoy their own culture, to practice their religion and speak their language. Just as they need not be nationals of citizens, they need not be permanent residents. Thus, migrant workers or even visitors in a State party constituting such minorities are entitled not to be denied the exercise of those rights (…) The existence of an ethnic, religious or linguistic minority in a given State party does not depend upon a decision by that State party but requires to be established by objective criteria.[17]

Concerning rights for a minority as a collective, the human right system is less clarifying although the question is of current interest. There exists no univocal definition in international law of the concept minority. It is even more difficult to get answers to the difference between minority and people. In one perspective minority can signal the difference in number between two or more groups in the same society. When talking about minority there are elements putting one group compared to others in an exceptional position based on for instance religion, sex, color, race, or national origin. The most general description of the concept minority in the international human rights discourse can be found in "The Declaration on the Rights of Persons belonging to National or Ethnic, Religious and Linguistic Minorities." *Article 1* states:

---

17. *Compilation of General Comments.*

1. States shall protect the existence and the national or ethnic, cultural, religious and linguistic identity of minorities within their respective territories and shall encourage conditions for the promotion of that identity.
2. States shall adopt appropriate legislative and other measures to achieve those ends.

According to *Article 2* minority is clarified as "national or ethnic, religious or linguistic minorities."

There has been developed some suggestions concerning criteria for a definition of "minority" or group including:[18]

- numerical inferiority
- socio-political non-dominance
- a distinctive language, religion or ethnic belonging
- a shared history, experience and a sense of solidarity
- nationality or citizen status.

For a distinctive religious group in a dominant, majority setting it is clear that the international law looks upon such a group as a minority and safeguards its existence as nationals or citizens in a specific society or State. This is may be the way chosen by communities and the state in Pakistan.

EITHER WAY OR (. . .)?

In some societies it may be enough to talk about equal nationals in a democratic society and thereby safeguarding all religious individuals and communities in their belief and practices. In other societies this seems not to be enough and there is need of more protection of vulnerable individuals and communities.

In the Middle East and in Pakistan many groups fit the category "minority" according to a human right perspective. "Compact minorities" have been used to characterize communities, which are in majority in a certain geographic area inside a state. The numerically large peoplegroups without a state or with an embryo to self-determination include the Kurds and what they call Kurdistan and the Palestinians on the West Bank and the Gaza Strip. Numerically inferior groups in power as the Alawites in Syria and earlier on the Maronites in Lebanon also belong

---

18. *Rights of Persons*; Thorberry, *International Law*.

The Use of the Concept Minority

to the concept of minority. At the same time they are a kind of compact minority in their respective areas of settlement. Also the Druze population and to some extent the Yezidis are compact minorities but in rather limited geographic areas.

Minorities according to the international interpretation are also religious or ethnic groups scattered in the different countries of the Middle East and Pakistan as Christians, Ismailites, Samaritans and followers of Baha'i as well as the Jews living in Muslim countries and Muslims in Israel as well as Hindus and Parsis in Pakistan. The Christian and the Muslim communities are divided into different shadings formed as sects and denominations reciprocally consisting of majorities respectively minorities.

All these communities/minorities in the Middle East and Pakistan are deeply rooted in national, ethnic, religious, and linguistic traditions. Whenever the treatment of one or several of these groups in any degree includes discrimination the relation between the majority and minorities will be problematic. Occasionally discrimination escalates to oppression and discrimination in politics, education and legislation.

So when using the international law it is possible to stick to the concept of equality of all individuals. But it is also possible to relate to the concept of minority. Or maybe they are parallel possibilities or can even go together in traditions with ambition to rely on equality, democracy, human rights, and freedom of religion.

4

Non-Muslim in Middle Eastern Muslim Societies

Guirguis Ibrahim Saleh

TODAY, MORE THAN AT any time, our region seems to be balanced upon the lip of a volcano. From the problem of Iran, to the blistering situations in Iraq, Palestine, and Sudan (Darfur), the disturbed situation in Syria and Egypt, and the situation in Lebanon after the Israeli attack that took place July 2006, there is a non stop aggression on human rights and dignity.

It is with much regret that the tense political environment in the whole region leaves no room for objective thinking. As we monitor events, listen to statements, and observe the positions adopted by those in power in the region and by those who do the endorsing from abroad, it becomes clear that we are unfortunately still living in the same troubled conditions.

LEBANON

The situation in Lebanon is particularly precarious. There is a general mood of despair, sadness and ambiguity at all levels, especially in light of recent political events. The fight at Nahr El Bared Palestinian Camp in 2007, besides the weekly bomb attacks and the car bombs blast, has made life for the Lebanese unbearable. The country is trapped in a struggle between regional and western powers. Its near future is unclear, which lead to more economic difficulties, increasing unemployment, and immigration.

IRAQ

From our close perspective, the conflict in Iraq is one targeted against the people. More than 2 million Iraqis have fled the violence engulfing their country, most to neighboring Jordan and Syria. The ethnic and sectarian conflicts, the lack of security and the increasing of bomb blasts, all constitute factors for an increasing trend of Christian emigration from this country.

Church leaders called on the Iraqi officials to put an end to the tragic situation and persecution that Christians in Iraq are enduring due to the constant threats and attacks against them.

In addition to being subjected to threats, killings, and protection payments, Christians are also being forced to flee from their own homes leaving everything behind. The armed militants then force the Christians to pay an "exit fee" of $200 per person and $400 per car.

In Dora, only the families that agree to give a daughter or sister in marriage to a Muslim can remain, which means that the entire nuclear family will progressively become Muslim. Analysts worry that the departure of the Christian community from Iraq, which has roots going back to antiquity, could make it more difficult to pacify the country.

At all levels of political life, the participation of Christians has been very limited in Iraq. Christians were denied access to superior political, governmental, or military positions.

JORDAN

Jordan can be considered as being somewhat typical and more Western in comparison to its Middle Eastern neighbors, having housed millions of refugees fleeing more dire conditions in their neighboring homelands. However, it still maintains the title of a predominantly Muslim nation and the label is not confined to religious preferences, but has leaked into various aspects of government. Courts are controlled by Muslims and persons of other faiths face a multitude of obstacles in achieving rights equal to those of their Muslim countrymen.

Jordan's indigenous Arab Christian minority is not in high spirits these days. Political uncertainty next door, both in Iraq and Palestine, and growing popular perceptions of a new global crusade being waged against Islam and Arab culture in the name of the "war on terror" are souring their mood. Both Christians and Muslims are outspoken critics of continued Israeli atrocities in the West Bank and the Gaza Strip and want to see the emergency of an independent Palestinian state. They also want to see an end to the American occupation of Iraq and a return of law and order, key factors that continue to encourage many Iraqi Christians to emigrate to the West.

SYRIA

Damascus was one of the first regions to receive Christianity during the ministry of Paul. There were more Christians in Damascus than anywhere else. After the military expansion of the Umayyed Empire into Syria and Anatolia, the teachings of Islam came into practice and many became Muslims.

Damascus is open to Christianity. Christians have churches all over the city. Masses are held every Sunday and civil servants are given the mornings off on Sunday mornings to allow them to attend church, even though Sunday is a working day in Syria. Schools in Christian-dominated districts have Saturday and Sunday as the weekend, while the official Syrian weekend falls on Friday and Saturday. Syrian Christians have their own courts that deal with civil cases like marriage, divorce and inheritance based on Biblical teachings. Christians engage in and enjoy every aspect of Syrian life. Syrian Christians are participants in the economic, academic, scientific, engineering, artistic, intellectual, entertainment, and political arenas of Syria. Many Syrian Christians are managers and directors in the public and private sectors, local administrators, members of the parliament, and ministers in the government. A number of Syrian Christians are also officers in the armed forces of Syria. As a result, Syrian Christians are generally viewed by other Syrians as an asset to the larger community.

EGYPT

Unfortunately, Egypt has recently experienced a rising sensitivity over religious issues. Although Christian-Muslim relations have generally been peaceful, there have been periodic outbreaks of violence, especially in southern Egypt, where the issue is particularly sensitive. Another source of trouble sparked off whit Coptic Christian attempts to build a new church.

All involved called for calm and for inter-faith dialogue in order to resolve outstanding differences. We believe that the tension between Egypt's Muslim majority and Coptic Christian minority rises whenever the country heads toward parliamentary elections.

So far, Islam is Egypt's official state religion and according to the constitution, legislation is loosely based on Islamic Shari'ah law.

Many challenges face Egyptian Christians. They complain of official discrimination, particularly at the local level, which lead to more economic difficulties, increasing unemployment and emigration. Copts also point to the under-representation of Christians in the government, army and police at the national level. Even so, Egypt has the highest number of Christian in the region.

UNITED ARAB EMIRATES

In Dubai Christians pray side by side but not always together. The presence of Christianity in the Gulf today is due primarily to the presence of migrant workers in the region. Arab workers from Palestine, Jordan, Lebanon, Syria, and Egypt have brought with them the Greek Orthodox, Greek Catholic, Roman Catholic, Syrian Orthodox, and Coptic churches, among others. Likewise, Christian migrant workers from India, the Philippines and other Asian countries also contribute to this diversity.

As in other parts of the Middle East, the primary organization aimed at cooperation among churches and at communication with government agencies is the Middle East Council of Churches (MECC). While the main headquarters of MECC is located in Beirut, one of the six MECC liaison offices is housed in the Gulf. Concern for migrant workers has become one of the highest priorities of the Middle East Council of Churches.

On Fridays, the Holy Trinity Church compound in Dubai is abuzz with worshipers from early morning until after nightfall. Some 10–11 000 members of more than 120 different Christian groups and congregations come here on the Emirates' weekly day of rest.

Services in more than a dozen tongues—including English and Arabic, but most of them South Asian—fill not only the main church from 6 am to 11 pm but the twenty-five other halls built around a central courtyard adorned with a Canterbury cross.

A vibrant church life may not be the first thing that comes to mind when thinking about the Gulf region, which is primarily Muslim. But in a way, the 3–4 million Christians in the region, almost all of whom came in search of work from around the globe, present a microcosm of Christianity and the challenges of church unity. The main area in which churches can do good work together is their care for the needs of migrant workers.

At the Holy Trinity compound, the Christian testimony is one of diversity in worship, from the solemnity of song to happy clapping. As one services ends, worshippers quickly rearrange what was a sober Protestant worship facility into an Orthodox sanctuary with icons and incense. Glory to God is proclaimed throughout the day in a variety of liturgies. It is worth noting also that in April 2007 HH Pope Shenouda III, Pope of Alexandria and Patriarch of the See of St. Mark, inaugurated a cathedral for the Coptic Orthodox in Abu Dhabi. The MECC General Secretary attended this ceremony as well.

In Dubai, as throughout the United Arab Emirates, Christians are free to practice their faith, but only within the limits of their church compounds or in the privacy of their homes. The foundation stone of Holy Trinity Church was laid in 1969 by Sheikh Rashid bin Said Al Maktoum, then ruler of Dubai, who had graciously granted the land to the Christians living in his sheikdom.

SAUDI ARABIA

The country is ruled by a monarchy with a legal system based on Islamic law (Shari'ah). Islam is the official religion and the law requires that all citizens be Muslim. Religious freedom is virtually non-existent. The public practice of non-Muslim religions is prohibited. Meetings of Christians can only take place informally in people's homes or at embassy compounds. The Government does not provide legal protection for freedom of religion and such protection does not exist in practice. The religious police see it as their main task to track down believers of other religions and to prevent gatherings of these believers.

Expatriate Christians live under strict surveillance. They can show no outward signs of being a Christian. They must be very careful especially at Christmas when the Mutawwa'in further step up their already tight surveillance. The Roman Catholic hierarchy has heightened calls from its Muslim counterparts for "reciprocity," demanding that the same religious freedom enjoyed by Muslims in the West should be granted to

Christian minorities in the Islamic world. They note that Europe's biggest mosque, built with Saudi funds, was opened in 1995 in Rome, just across the river from the Vatican.

It is believed that negotiations to open the first Catholic Church in Saudi Arabia will soon begin as the number of Catholics resident in Saudi Arabia has risen to over 800,000 due to the immigration of workers from places like the Philippines and India, as well as from Palestine, Lebanon, and Iraq.

PALESTINE AND ISRAEL

Christians have deep roots in the land—Palestine and Israel. The great majority of Christians are of indigenous stock. Their native language is Arabic. Many trace their history to the early church in Palestine.

The Christian population in Palestine has decreased due to the smaller Christian birthrate and the higher rate of emigration among Christians.

Palestinian Christians appeal to the conscience of the West, and to the government of the United States, that Palestinian Christianity may suffer if justice and peace are not implemented in Israel-Palestine soon. The fundamental problem for Palestinian Christians is the same as that for all Palestinians: the occupation of land and the brutal Israeli measures against the entire Palestinian community. Thus, Palestinians and Israelis will continue to suffer insecurity, economic deprivation, and death from the inhumane status quo of occupation until Israel complies with UN resolutions 242 and 338.

MIGRATION

Throughout the entire Middle East, Christian communities have shrunk to a miniscule portion of their former robust selves. Why has there been a great Christian emigration from the Middle East? For sure some have left to avoid the endless acts of violence and conflicts, while others have left for economic and political reasons.

Consequently, Christian migration away from the Middle East becomes a serious issue, as it affects Christian presence in a significant way. Numbers of Christians in the Middle East are diminishing, but the decline differs from country to country depending on socio-economic and political climate.

MIDDLE EAST COUNCIL OF CHURCHES

Therefore, the MECC must be sensitive to current changes in the region and be responsive to the needs of Middle Eastern Christians and citizens. Nevertheless, the topics raised in this conference are priorities in the Council's agenda.

Ever since its establishment in 1974, MECC has been working through its units and programs on maintaining the dignity of humanity, the acceptance of the other, and respect for plurality in society.

The Council, which is the venue where local churches meet, might realize through its church committees the objectives it was established to fulfill, which are:

> Provision of humanitarian services and promotion and support of a systematic Christian-Muslim dialogue aimed at creating mutual understanding for the consolidation of peace and good relations among peoples for the benefit of Humanity.

The significance of the Christian-Muslim encounter and dialogue in the Middle East is based on the deeply entrenched roots of co-existence in the region. Christian-Muslim dialogue is one of the Council's high priorities and an integral part of its work.

Over the years and given recent events and changes in the region, and in terms of daily life and shared destiny, the Christian-Muslim dialogue has become indispensable.

All issues are reduced to one: we live together in one land and cherish hope for one bright future. This is especially true since dialogue equally provides both Christians and Muslims with a common sense of Arab citizenship and identity in the Middle East.

Among the Council's identified goals is developing and strengthening a systematic dialogue aimed at achieving mutual understanding for consolidating peace and creating good relations between people for the benefit of humanity. Through the Christian-Muslim dialogue program, the Council endeavors to achieve the following:

- Contributing to the establishment of Arab Christianity as a central partner in the Christian-Muslim dialogue worldwide.
- Using this dialogue as a means for getting to know Islam and Muslims circumstances as well as acquainting Muslims with Christianity and

the circumstances of Christians. The Council also endeavors to keep religion away from becoming a cause of divisions and war, but rather a factor of peace and cooperation that is based on a common sense of citizenship.

- Eliminating inherited pre-judgment and mistaken opinions of each other acquired by ignorance.
- Acquiring knowledge of the mutual intellectual grounds and moral values.
- Joining efforts in shouldering responsibilities toward maintaining a healthy community where humanistic values are faced with great challenges.
- Working on respecting equality among citizens in a pluralistic community in which freedom based on democratic foundations is embraced. This is a way of achieving unity in diversity, where everyone is committed to issues of mutual destiny, basic human needs, human rights, justice and peace in an open civil society.

Christian-Muslim encounter for dialogue is unique to this region. Although Christianity was preached to the whole world, this is still the place where Christian pilgrims from around the world come to visit holy sites. It is also from this region that Islam spread out to the whole world and it is still the place where all Muslims come to observe their religious duty of pilgrimage.

Dialogue is a mission that calls for getting to know the other and accepting them, not withstanding differences. It is a mission aimed at achieving justice, spreading peace and defending human rights. The consultations carried out in the Christian-Muslim dialogue aim at identifying mutual intellectual areas and values, and jointly shouldering responsibilities for maintaining a healthy society in places where human values are faced with great threats.

Given the great significance and the sensitivity of this approach this dialogue between religious leaders can have a positive impact on all levels of the community, especially at the youth level. It can lead to a healthy upbringing and to the realization of good relations with our compatriots. This emphasizes our effective presence in the region. We, as Christians, do not represent an inert part of society. We are active and interactive. We constitute an influential element in the procedure of events.

Our role as a council of churches gains an added significance in this beloved Middle East as we keep in mind the deteriorating political circumstances as a result of the American support for Israel and its aggressions while overlooking the oppressions practiced against the Palestinian people. These circumstances have been exacerbated by the occupation of Iraq, the despotic treatment of its land and people and last, but not least, the offensive cartoons directed against Islam. Some have tried, whether out of ignorance or out of malice, to create an erroneous impression of this imperialistic aggression propagating it as being in part a Christian aggression. Needless to say, Christianity has nothing to do with these actions. The Christians of the Middle East were the first targeted by those intent on tearing the fabric of kinship that binds Middle Eastern communities together.

We are trying to correct this delineated picture for fear it might get rooted in the minds of some engendering hatred and fear of Christians on all levels. We are working on this with all our partners, councils of churches in America and Europe who support our Arab causes and who are attempting to persuade their governments to put an end to the injustice afflicting our region. These councils have condemned the occupation their governments have taken part. We, as the Middle East Council of Churches, do emphasize through our work that Christianity is a religion of love, peace, and justice. It is far from hatred, war, injustice, and terrorism.

These circumstances call on us to believe that Christian-Muslim convergence and interaction are requisite for the benefit of people in our Middle East Region, especially as we work together with youth to inculcate in them a common perception of values such as love, mercy and true faith so as to withstand atheism and the ills that afflict our societies because of globalization and its repercussions.

This kind of cooperation will be a model from which Western countries with expanding Muslim communities, already well integrated in their societies, will benefit.

The Middle East Council of Churches actually started the new phase of its activities for Christian-Muslim dialogue after the eighth Assembly by working on two levels:

- Christian-Muslim encounter for dialogue of religious leaders.
- Youth encounters for deepening roots of shared living.

The Council has had several activities in this domain according to the instructions of the commission of Christian-Muslim dialogue appointed by the executive committee.

INTER-FAITH DIALOGUE

Within the framework of Christian-Muslim Dialogue the Middle East Council of Churches and the International Islamic Forum for Dialogue (IIFD) signed a dialogue agreement on July 16, 2004 in which common objectives were identified as follows:

- Whereas each of us believes that religion is the essential component of the educational upbringing of the human generation and the strongest source for the formation of their culture and behavior.
- Whereas every one of us emphasizes that the divine religious values and principles are the safe and active source for achieving the best for individuals and communities.
- Whereas we have committed ourselves to shoulder responsibilities toward our generations and communities and toward all humanity for the realization of justice, peace, stability, good development, prosperity and secure coexistence among individuals, national and international communities.
- Whereas every one of us has a true and sincere desire to cooperate in establishing and promoting a culture of respect of human life, human dignity, and maintaining the environment and mutual human brotherhood and benefits (...)

Finally, I would like to state here that our dialogue is not just another one to be added to many other world dialogues whose real role and objectives are well known to all. Our dialogue is carried out within our one home, in an atmosphere filled with the fragrance of rapprochement and communication. Our aim is to give a good impression to our people and effectively foster in them love for one another.

However, it is vital that the Christians of the Middle East revitalize their own cultural role that has characterized their modern history. It is no exaggeration to say that Christians of the Middle East are indispensable to a democratic and pluralistic Arab World. Thus, their presence is as important to the outside world as to their own countrymen.

May God almighty bless our objectives and our good intentions, and may He grant you good health and peace of mind, and may the Lord grant your homelands security and peace.

5

Faith Based Organizations and the Configuration of Civil Society in the MENA-perspective

Johan Gärde

WELCOME TO THE REGION of GONGOs, DONGOs, MONGOs, CONGOs and why not M(n)ONGOs?[1] This chapter will attempt to discuss why the region of the Middle East and North Africa (MENA), is full of M(n)Ongos, especially among different minority groups and communities and their relations, interaction and context and why their impact often is so fragmented and limited in a wider and broader perspective. I will also attempt to analyze and grasp the difficulties in defining what is a "minority," why some of them do not consider themselves to be minorities, or why they might not be classified as minorities despite the fact that most scholars would argue that they are. My main concern is how minorities organize themselves in the public spheres, their interaction with the state, private sectors and other confessional groups, social movements and organizations in the arena of civil society. I am also proposing a set of guidelines and benchmarks of an enabling civil society, based on available research and data from the MENA-region.

---

1. Governmental-Organized NGOs, Donor-Organized NGOs, Muslim-Organized NGOs, Christian-Organized NGOs, my own NGO, where "n" stands for not organized. Cf. Carapico, "NGOs, INGOs."

DEFINING THE GEOGRAPHICAL AND DEMOGRAPHICAL BOUNDARIES OF THE MENA-REGION

Neither viability nor stability are the main ingredients of today's Iraq, the Middle East, the MENA-region or what the G8-group and powerful nations of today have described as the *Broader Middle East and North Africa(MENA)-region* (BMENA), which includes countries from Mauritania in the west to Pakistan in the east, Turkey in the north to Somalia and Sudan in the south. And what is the MENA-region? Does it "exist"? What do those countries have in common? For the sake of clarity, in this chapter, MENA denotes for all the twenty-two member states of the League of Arab States, plus Turkey and Iran. Official UN and Arab League data indicates that the total population of the twenty-two "Arab Nations" is 285 million.[2] The total population of this geographical area plus Turkey (71 million) and Iran (65 million) is approximately 422 million and almost half of the citizens are under the age of fifteen.[3] The region is divided into the high income Gulf countries, the majority being middle-income countries in North Africa and the Middle East, and the so-called "Least Developed Countries," or LDCs.

MINORITIES IN THE MENA-REGION

Who is the majority and what kind of minorities do we have in this part of the world? The dominant religion is Sunni Islam, compromising approximately 77% of the total population. The minority Shiites in the MENA-region make up approximately 15% of the whole, although they are the majority in Iran (90%), Iraq (60%), Bahrain (75%), as well as being the largest confessional group in Lebanon (approx 40%).[4] The issues of classification of communities, definition of minorities, ethnicity and belonging are complex and controversial in academic terms but also from a more practical and operational view. Membership and numbers are highly sensitive and delicate issues. They are also political issues: matters of power and authority. The following figure illustrates some examples of majority-minority identities using the components of "Arab" and "Muslim" as points of departure:

---

2. *Arab Human* ... 2002, 143.
3. *World Factbook*. The figures for Iran and Turkey are from July 2007.
4. Cf. Beehner, "Shia Muslims."

Faith Based Organizations

FIGURE 1. Muslim and Arab Identity and Minority Group Identity in the Middle East

Muslim and Arab	Muslim and non-Arab
Majority: Sunnites in Saudi Arabia *Minority*: Shiite Arabs in Iran	*Majority*: Iranian (Persian) Shiites in Iran *Minorities*: Kurds in Syria
Non-Muslim and Arab	Non-Muslim and not Arab
Majority: Maronite Christians in some areas of Lebanon *Minority*: Palestinian Christians in the Palestinian Territories	*Majority*: Israeli Jews in Israel *Minority*: Armenian Christians in Jerusalem; Assyrians in Iraq

There are indeed difficulties in classifying some confessional minority group as "Arabs." What is it indeed to be an "Arab"? Is a Maronite Christian in Lebanon an Arab? Most would probably say "no," that they have a distinct identity and that they lived in Lebanon long before the Arabs and Muslims, etc.[5] The key issues are of community and identity, which would be defined in textbooks and encyclopedias as follows:

> A social group whose members live in a specific locality, share government, and have a common heritage,

- Joint possession,
- Similar or common character: community of interest,
- The public or society.

Bernard Lewis, in his famous book *The Multiple Identities of the Middle East*, argues that there are three kinds or sets of identities in the Middle East:[6]

Primary category:	Involuntary
Secondary category:	Compulsory
Third category:	Voluntary

Identities belonging to the primary category are acquired at birth. 1. Blood; The family, the clan, the tribe and developing into the ethnic nation. 2.

---

5. Cf. remarks by Christian Politicians such as former Maronite President Bechir Gemayel who refused the positions of second-class citizens for Christians, or what he called "dhimmitude" in the Arab World. He was killed in 1982.

6. Lewis, *The Multiple Identities*.

Place; Often, but not always coinciding with the first and sometimes in conflict with it. Village or neighborhood, district or quarter, province or city, developing into a nation. 3. Religious Community; Often subdivided into sects.

Secondary category identities are described as:

> Allegiance to a ruler, the obedience to the sovereign; the head of state or of a department, the governor, the administrator, or the headman of a village.

Third category of identities:

> In modern times, under the influence of the West a new kind of identity is evolving: freely chosen cohesion and loyalty of voluntary associations: "Civil Society."

Why bring up the question of minorities in the Middle East? The answer is all about belonging, identity, and in the end citizenship. Let me give an example from Iraq: "I belong to a minority of a minority of a minority."

This statement came from a friend of mine, an Iraqi from Baghdad, who is Roman-Catholic and member of the Latin Church in Iraq. The Latin Church in Iraq? Is he a real Iraqi? What kind of minority group is that? Are he and his community a part of Iraqi civil society? Do they belong to what is considered one of the established groups, sects or minorities of Iraq? Does civil exist in today's Iraq?

He belongs to a community of some 2,000 members. The Latin Church in Iraq is a minority Church within the Oriental Catholic family in Iraq, where the Chaldeans are the biggest Christian group. And it is a minority within the Christian sects and denominations in the Arab World (where the Orthodox churches are bigger than the combined eight Oriental Catholic Churches in size and numbers) and also a minority in the confessional fabric of Iraq, where Christians today constitutes between 2–3% of the total population according to official figures[7] and probably less than 1.2% if we take into account the emigration of recent years due to the lack of security and stability. A minority of a minority of a minority. But still 100% Iraqi! My Iraqi friend defended his motherland in the Iraqi war against Iran in the 1980s and spent over 10 years in the frontlines. He is an Iraqi nationalist, member of a prominent family from a middle-class area in one of the well-respected areas of Baghdad.

---

7. Barret, *World Christian*.

Moreover he is one of the few Iraqis who contributed to the creation of one of the rare autonomous Iraqi civil society organizations or faith based organizations under the Saddam-regime. At the time there were less than 20 registered civil society organizations in Iraq. Several of them belonged to different Christian confessional groups and ecumenical networks, such as the Middle East Council of Churches (MECC) and Caritas.

Yes indeed, my friend is a real Iraqi. When the media and the world describe Iraq we usually hear about the Sunnis, the Shiites and the Kurds. We hear about divisions and the risk that Iraq will be divided into three separate nations. Is the "Iraq" of today a viable state and what happens to people, communities and the arena of formal and informal organizations when everything is moving around you? The map of communities, minorities, sects and groups is more complex and subtle and is a matter of both survival and frustrations in Iraq and many other countries in the Middle East and beyond. Just ask the Mandeans, the Jazidis and the disappearing Chaldeans and Assyrians of Iraq.

THE CHRISTIANS IN THE MENA-REGION

In this presentation, I will limit my study mainly to the 26 million Christians living in the MENA-region and how they relate, participate and take part in what we call "civil society." You might be surprised by this number:

TABLE 1: Christian membership data in the MENA-region

	1900	1995	2005
Egypt	9,571,000	10,345,789	13,710,000
Sudan	2,375	4,490,000	4,920,955
Lebanon	317,400	1,604,000	1,758,354
Syria	274,000	1,145,200	1,262,719
Saudi-Arabia	50	660,000	789,065
Iraq	144,110	671,500	740,778
Turkey	3,091,530	375,700	388,757
Iran	116,200	325,000	363,054
Israel	29,700	259,000	297,146
Libya	168,500	175,498	292,300
Jordan	14,600	227,000	273,889

United Arab Emirates	50	237,300	270,244
Kuwait	200	210,800	249,546
Morocco	161,700	175,435	248,000
Palestine	30,300	168,900	189,641
Algeria	85,500	90,952	159,000
Oman	20	104,110	124,127
Somalia	600	115,000	101,881
Tunisia	50,000	51,566	80,000
Bahrain	200	56,400	64,475
Qatar	-	38,400	39,259
Yemen	4,500	27,000	32,192
Djibouti	100	29,350	28,516
Somaliland	-	7,650	8,401
Mauritania	6,520	6,569	7,580
Comoros	100	6,150	7,192
Total	**14,071,155**	**21,606,264**	**26,409,076**

Generally speaking, studies and surveys conducted by scholars and well reputed institutions such as the World Christian Encyclopedia should also be matched by the reported figures from the respective churches and ecumenical institutions.[8] This table has been sorted according to the size of each Christian community in the respective countries in 2005. Compiling these figures from a total of twenty-six countries in the MENA-region, our first conclusion would be that the Christian population is approximately 5% of the total population.[9] Two countries in Africa, Egypt and Sudan, count for more than 71% of the reported Christians in the MENA-region. Countries with historical high numbers of Christians in the Middle East make up only approximately 20% of the total Christians in the area. If we would sort the same table according to size in the year of 1900 we would get the following result:

---

8. Cf. "Guide: Christians."

9. The World Christian Database would give other figures, compiled both from governmental sources and church estimates. See *World Christian*.

Faith Based Organizations

TABLE 2: Christian membership data in the MENA-region

	1900	1995	2005
Egypt	9,571,000	10,345,789	13,710,000
Turkey	3,091,530	375,700	388,757
Lebanon	317,400	1,604,000	1,758,354
Syria	274,000	1,145,200	1,262,719
Libya	168,500	175,498	292,300
Morocco	161,700	175,435	248,000
Iraq	144,110	671,500	740,778
Iran	116,200	325,000	363,054
Algeria	85,500	90,952	159,000
Tunisia	50,000	51,566	80,000
Palestine	30,300	168,900	189,641
Israel	29,700	259,000	297,146
Jordan	14,600	227,000	273,889
Mauritania	6,520	6,569	7,580
Yemen	4,500	27,000	32,192
Sudan	2,375	4,490,000	4,920,955
Somalia	600	115,000	101,881
Kuwait	200	210,800	249,546
Bahrain	200	56,400	64,475
Djibouti	100	29,350	28,516
Comoros	100	6,150	7,192
Saudi-Arabia	50	660,000	789,065
United Arab Emirates	50	237,300	270,244
Oman	20	104,110	124,127
Qatar	-	38,400	39,259
Somaliland	-	7,650	8,401
Total	14,071,155	21,606,264	26,409,076

There are several interesting patterns to comment upon, particularly: the dramatic decrease in the number of Christians in Turkey (or what was the heartland of the former Ottoman empire) and in North Africa; the slow increase of Christians in countries with historically high proportions of non-Muslims, such as Lebanon, Syria, Iraq, Jordan, and Palestine; the sharp increase of mainly Asian and African Christians moving to the Gulf countries (see table below); and, the high increase of Christians in other parts of Africa than the Maghreb.

The following table will illustrate the situation for Christians in the Middle East, excluding the Gulf states; countries where the Christian population has been significant since the birth of Christ:

TABLE 3: Christian Membership in the Middle East (excl. the Gulf states)

Middle East excl. the Gulf states	1900	1995	2005
Lebanon	317,400	1,604,000	1,758,354
Jordan	14,600	227,000	273,889
Iraq	144,110	671,500	740,778
Iran	116,200	325,000	363,054
Egypt	9,571,000	10,345,789	13,710,000
Palestine	30,300	168,900	189,641
Israel	29,700	259,000	297,146
Syria	274,000	1,145,200	1,262,719
Total	10,499,210	14,748,384	18,597,586

Outside Egypt, the number of Christians remaining in the Middle East (excluding the Gulf states) is probably less than 5 million. The most dramatic decrease is probably occurring in Iraq, where the number of Christians is probably less than 300,000 in 2008. That is a little bit more than double the number in 1900, but in proportion to the Iraqi population the Christians probably comprise less than 2% of the population. There are probably more Assyrians living in the Swedish city of Södertälje than in the province of Nineve and northern Iraq combined. Another trend is the rise of Christians in the Gulf countries in the last 100 years:

TABLE 4: Christian Membership in the Gulf States

The Gulf states	1900	1995	2005
Saudi-Arabia	50	660,000	789,065
Qatar	-	38,400	39,259
Bahrain	200	56,400	64,475
United Arab Emirates	50	237,300	270,244

Kuwait	200	210,800	249,546
Yemen	4,500	27,000	32,192
Total	**6,900**	**1,231,895**	**1,446,786**

Most "native" Christians of Middle Eastern descent would not consider these Christians as indigenous Christians belonging to the region. They are considered as foreigners and aliens despite the fact that many of them have been living in the Middle East for two or even three generations. As citizen rules are very strict, most Christians remain as permanent residents or with work permits. Several countries in the Gulf region are more liberal and permit right of religion and cult, which is also changing the landscape of social associations and organizations, i.e. civil society organizations among the African- and Asian- born Christians in countries such as Qatar, Kuwait and the United Arab Emirates.

CIVIL SOCIETY

"Civil society" has become the panacea in order to generate development, democratic reforms, people's participation and good governance. NGOs are the mantra for policy-makers, donor agencies and governments when dealing with social affairs in general and social change in particular. There is however a danger to view civil society organizations (CSOs) as purely instrumental:

> (...) on the way to bigger political and economic goals in order to further a number of objectives in the spheres of democratization, human rights and good governance.[10]

Civil society organizations do not exist only because the state is not delivering: their role should not only be reduced to a replacement for the failure of the state.

There is a general consensus by scholars, analysts and practitioners that the increased importance of CSOs in the development and humanitarian sectors is part of a global trend[11]: "The dramatic expansion in the size, scope and capacity of CSOs around the globe over the past decade has had a major impact (...)" on major multilateral and bilateral institu-

---

10. Roy, "The Transformation."
11. Salamon et al., *Global Civil Society*; Salamon et al., *Social Origins*; Howell and Pearce, *Civil Society*; Kandil, "Egypt."

tions and policy makers in "the development business."[12] There have been several global attempts to quantify and measure the growing importance of the civil society sector with its impact on employment, income and service provision[13] and the associational relations in development processes.[14] This worldwide trend, with a special emphasis and interest on the "third sector," NGOs and civil society seems also to include regions like the Middle-East and North Africa (MENA):

> Until the late 1980s, there were few if any significant scholarly studies or journalistic accounts of what we now call NGOs in the Arab/Muslim Middle East.[15]

It has also been argued that:

> (. . .) governments throughout the region have become more aggressive and are employing tactics to undermine and discredit NGOs' efforts.[16]

The increased focus on *accountability, governance* and *transparency* gives CSOs a greater role when it comes to renewing and developing the public sector. The changes can also be noted in the Middle East, where the war in Iraq has put additional pressure on most governments in the MENA-region to re-think their current policies, organizational set-ups, as well as their limited inability to deliver social welfare and wellbeing to the citizens. International polls show that CSOs enjoy greater public trust than governments and private corporations.[17] NGO accountability is also crucial in parts of the world where legal frameworks and/or external controls are weak or nearly non-existent.

There is, however, evidence that many new NGOs and CSOs in the MENA-region are facing increased legal and political hurdles and restrictions of different kinds when it comes to registration, funding and implementation of social programs and projects.[18] The consequence is that the

12. *Issues and Options.*

13. Salamon, and Anheier, *In Search of*; Salamon, and Anheier, *The Third World's.*

14. Putnam, *Making Democracy*; Fukuyama, *End of History*; cf. Howell and Pearce, *Civil Society.*

15. Carapico, "NGOs, INGOs."

16. Pitner, "NGO Dilemma."

17. *Issues and Options.*

18. *Arab Human . . . 2002; Arab Human . . . 2003; Arab Human . . . 2004;* Gärde, *NGO-Law.*

Faith Based Organizations

civil society sector shows signs of stagnation in several countries in the Arab World, with few new registrations and/or incorporated CSOs or just a modest growth of new NGOs and CSOs. One way out for many social associations is to work under the protection of religious authorities. A possible effect is the dramatic growth of new faith based organizations and social movements. Restricted by their respective religious leaders and Shari'ah law, many social and political organizations are working underground and are facing growing oppression from their respective governments. The situation is even more difficult for NGOs active in advocacy and the promotion of human rights, whose actions are considered "political" and thus "illegal." These governmental measures are not always based on the rule of law and are considered to be against international human rights and standards.[19]

There are many challenges to face and questions to be answered. The first issues are related to the concept and definition of civil society in general terms: How is "civil society" being defined, in which context and by whom? What is the actual role of civil society? How is civil society being viewed? What is an NGO? What role are they playing in civil society?

The second major area of concern is how to apply those theoretical concepts in a given (and changing!) context, like the MENA-region in general and specific Arab nations like Syria, Iraq, and Palestine, in particular. Is it relevant and possible to apply the concepts of "civil society" in the Arab World and beyond? What are the lessons learnt in the region? How is civil society being viewed and what kind of civil societies do we have in the MENA-region today (2005)? How are Arab NGOs performing and evolving in the areas of service delivery (meeting needs) and advocacy (influencing public policies and addressing inequalities)?[20]

Definitions

There are many operational definitions used to describe what "civil society" is and what it stands for. A common description is the following:

> Social institutions that operate outside the confines of the market and the state. Known variously as the "non-profit," the "voluntary," the "civil society," the "third," or the "independent" sector.[21]

---

19. Latham, *Non-Governmental*; Gärde, *NGO-Law*; "Arab Charter."
20. Cf. *Making Services Work*.
21. Salamon et al., *Global Civil Society*.

There are six fundamental criteria to consider in order to label an association or an entity "part" of civil society:[22]

- Voluntary
- Self-ruled
- Non-governmental
- Not-for profit
- Public and/or social benefit
- Organized (formal or informal)

Boundaries and the Spheres of Civil Society

Traditionally, the civil society sector is being labeled "the third sector," almost as a complimentary to the public and private sectors (first and second). There is however a growing number of scholars arguing for a more comprehensive analysis of the interaction between the different social sectors of society where the main focus should be the social well-being of its citizens (see below). In essence, civil society cannot only be reduced to NGOs and some particular kinds of associations.[23]

Informal social networks. According to some scholars the sphere of civil society excludes informal social networks, such as the extended family, the tribe and the clan. Others, including practitioners from the South, would question that assumption and also include the family and other kinds of informal social networks.

Political parties. The political parties as such are usually not considered to be part of civil society. They are however crucial and fundamental vehicles in the democratic process of every country.

Religious groups. There has been a debate by some academicians whether or not to include all kinds of religious groups in the notion of civil society. Other scholars conclude that there is a growing importance of faith based organizations in the social and developmental sectors.

Extremist, racist groups and anti-democratic forces. All groups and associations should not be considered as part of civil society, even if they fulfill the six criteria above. Among them are xenophobic, racist, and violent groups using anti-democratic means.

22. Salamon et al., *Global Civil Society.*
23. Svedberg and Trägårdh, *Sweden.*

Faith Based Organizations

Common Good Criteria and Member-based Organizations

Some countries have introduced very strict criteria to measure what constitutes "common-good," which an association should comply with, before being organizations are able to get tax-exemptions and other benefits from the state. Membership-based organizations that only fit the interest of their own members are in that perspective not contributing to the "common-good."

Associations involved with advocacy work and issues related to policy and what might be considered politics have sometimes also been excluded from the right to register or be incorporated as "charities."

Current Trends in Arab Countries Regarding Civil Society

Few countries and governments are today openly opposed to "civil society" and most would promote NGOs in various key areas of public interest. That is also the case in the Arab World and the wider MENA-region: Iraq has approximately 3,000–6,000 registered NGOs, Iran possesses a thriving civil society with over 8,000 NGOs, Egypt more than 27,000 NGOs, and the Palestinian Territories have approximately 1,200 NGOs. It has been reported by Arab researchers that the increase in the numbers of CSOs has been dramatic in some of the Gulf countries 1990–99: Yemen (83%), Qatar (71%), Bahrain (46%); but also North Africa: Morocco (58%), Tunisia (41%); and the Middle East: Palestine (47%) and Jordan (40%). In Sudan it was reported that 74% of all CSOs were registered during the period 1990–2004.[24] According to Amani Kandil, currently there are approximately 233 000 NGOs in the Arab world.[25]

The Proportion of CSOs in the Arab World and Beyond

If Syria's current level of civil society organizations is analyzed in a comparative perspective with other MENA-countries, the conclusion is that that number of Syrian CSOs is among the lowest in the Arab World and can be classified as "low level density." A typology of CSOs into three categories (high level density, middle level density and low level density of CSO/population) gives the following result:

---

24. Arab Network for NGOs.
25. MoSA-workshop on Civil Society, February 2005.

TABLE 5: Size and Proportion of Civil Society Organizations in the MENA-region[26]

Country	Population	Number of Civil Society Organizations	Proportion of Population (persons per organization)	Organizations per 1,000 inhabitants
High Level Density				
Algeria	33,333,216	58,000	574	1.74
Morocco	33,757,175	30,000[27]	1,125	0.89
Lebanon	3,925,502	2,500–5,000	785–1,570	0.64–1.27
Tunisia	10,276,158	6,700	1,533	0.65
Middle Level Density				
Bahrain	708,573[28]	321	2,207	0.45
Egypt	80,335,036	26,594	3,021	0.33
Jordan	6,053,193	2,000	3,027	0.33
Palestine	4,018,332	1,150	3,494	0.27
Low Level Density				
Iraq	27,499,638	600–6,000[29]	4,583–45,833	0.022–0.22
Iran	65,397,521	8,000	8,175	0.12
Libya	6,036,914[30]	400	15,093	0.066
Kuwait	2,505,559[31]	103	24,326	0.04
Syria	19,314,747	516	37,432	0.027
United Arab Emirates	4,444,011	113	39,328	0.025
Saudi Arabia	27,601,038[32]	230	120,005	0.008
Other				
Sweden	9,031,088	170,000–195,000	53–46	18.9–21.7
Turkey	71,158,647	152,360[33]	467	2.14[34]

26. CIVICUS; *Civil Society and Governance*; Nasr, *Arab Civil Society*; Kandil, "Egypt"; Tabbaa, *Civil Society*; Hammami et al. *Civil Society*.

27. Nasr, *Arab Civil Society*.

28. Includes 235,108 non-nationals (July 2007 est.).

29. Registered in Baghdad and in Erbil. Figures include estimates from UNDP and Iraqi sources at a Save the Children UK Workshop in Amman, July 2005. From Iraqi sources at a Folke Bernadotte Workshop in Sweden, January 2008, the figure of 6,000 NGOs were launched.

30. Includes 166,510 non-nationals (July 2007 est.).

31. Includes 1,291,354 non-nationals (July 2007 est.).

32. Includes 5,576,076 non-nationals (July 2007 est.).

33. *Promotion of Cooperation*.

34. This figure is probably higher as the population in the table is from 2007 and the registered NGOs from 2001.

Faith Based Organizations

Current Trends and Challenges Facing Civil Society and NGOs in the MENA-region

The following issues are some of the important dimensions that NGOs are facing when getting organized. The MENA-region is changing and facing new challenges. The external context, the surrounding society and the way it is being ruled by governments, will directly influence civil society. A thriving civil society will also affect the state and there are different theories arguing that a strong civil society will diminish the role of the state. Conservative observers would even ideologically place CSOs in opposition to, and as a possible replacement of, certain governmental functions. Study of civil society is also the study of power-relations in society: "Power is a relational idea."[35] The state has a central role and is also considered the most important actor in improving development and building democracy. Civil society does not exist only because the state is not delivering: it cannot be seen as a replacement for the failings of the state.

Totalitarianism  Open Society

In some countries like Syria, NGOs are facing the prospects of becoming more regulated, controlled, and marginalized if the old system of total control and social monopoly by the state prevails. In that case, there will be little or no space for civil society and modern NGOs. In another case, if Arab and Oriental authorities will build up a new strategic framework around an amended NGO-law, which would facilitate the registration, functioning and financing of NGOs, countries like Syria and Libya would become more open societies with flourishing CSOs.

Formal  Non-formal

In several countries, there are few registered and formalized associations (less than 600) but quite strong informal social entities in the neighborhoods and countryside through extended families, clans and communities. It is important:

> (...) to take into account informal and unregistered organizations of civil society that carry tremendous weight in social change.[36]

35. Roy, "The Transformation."
36. Roy, "The Transformation."

Primary and secondary identities (blood, family, citizenship and religion), which are involuntary and compulsory in nature, are more important for an individual than making a free choice and becoming a member of an association (other than the party—or related governmental controlled groups).[37]

Top-down ←——————————→ Bottom-up

The question is also what kind of future associations will be active in MENA? What kind of organizational expressions will the future NGOs have? How will they be governed and by whom? What sort of management-structures? Will they have a participatory approach which will include the concerned stakeholders, the members and the target groups? Will they be ruled by some few individuals from the top or will the people at the bottom (the poor and marginalized) have a say?[38]

Religious ←——————————→ Secular

Faith based organizations (FBOs), Islamic and Christian charities, are playing central roles in civil society in the Middle East. That is normal as religion is a major factor that influences all aspects, dimensions and sectors of society in the Arab World. Religion can be part of the problem, but also part of the solution. Many FBOs are delivering excellent social services in key areas that benefit the poor. There are also a growing number of secular NGOs, often in collaboration with FBOs, active in civil society in the MENA-region. There are countries with secular governments, but with strong support for the different religious communities. A more open civil society might lead to a growing number of FBOs (Islamic charities) and/or secular NGOs. Social policies need to be elaborated which give incentives for inter-confessional and non-sectarian FBOs as well as actions which will put need before creed.

Development ←——————————→ Charity

Most associations in the MENA-region tend to be charity-oriented. They are often linked to different kinds of communities, i.e. community- and/

---

37. Cf. Lewis, *The multiple identities*.
38. Chambers, *Whose Reality*.

or faith-based. Their interests are quite narrow.[39] Their actions primarily serve their respective members. In that sense, the public benefits are quite marginal as the constituency is reduced to a small number of people. The charity organizations are often constituted by volunteers and are involved with traditional relief and emergency activities, through distribution and individual assistance. Modern NGOs active with development projects and programs are something rare in many countries. There are a lot of obstacles, regulations and policies that have made it quite impossible for NGOs to function. A new legal framework may open the way for a new dynamic approach, which would benefit different sectors including the public and private sectors.

Volunteer  Professional

Volunteering is one of the key ingredients in civil society. Most, if not all, NGOs have active volunteers who are carrying out the core of the activities. They are giving thousands of hours of their time are committed to their respective organizations, share the mission of "their association," and often contribute financially to the activities. All this is very positive and should be encouraged. In the Syrian case, a more professional and focused civil society sector is needed. Most young people have not even considered that there could be a career opportunity working with an NGO. The third (not-for profit) sector is one of the fastest growing in the whole world. The NGO sector is a major economic and social force in the world. It has been reported that by the mid-1990s, this sector accounted for:

- more than 1.2 trillion USD in expenditure,
- had more than 31 million employees and
- six times more paid employees than work in the largest private firm in each of the countries studied by a world-wide comparative study of the non-profit sector.[40]

Education, social services, and health account for 73% of the total non-profit paid employments in Western Europe.[41] Corresponding data for the Arab World is not available. The revenues funding the NGO sector come

39. Cf. *Making Services Work*.
40. Cf. *Global Civil Society At-a-Glance*.
41. *Global Civil Society At-a-Glance*.

from the public sector, private donations and through fees and charges. Employment in non-profit organizations has a tendency to grow much faster than overall employment in both developing and developed countries. In some countries, this growth is more than three times faster.[42] In order to respond to these needs, a focus on human resources is needed, with a clear vision for a more professional NGO-sector, which may create new jobs and opportunities for the Arab youth.

Urban  Rural

One important consideration is also where the NGOs of a country are located and their geographical areas of action. It is important to emphasize the significance of a well-balanced NGO-presence in both the urban and rural settings, in the capital, but also in other cities, villages and regions. Special considerations should be given to marginalized, remote and poor areas and the organization and involvement of the concerned communities in these areas. Formalized NGOs tend to be more of an urban phenomenon penetrating mainly middle-class sectors and already well-informed citizens. The challenge is the participation and involvement of a wider range of constituencies in rural and underdeveloped areas.

Conservative ⟵⟶ Progressive

There are different kinds of NGOs representing a variety of ideologies and political views. Some of the NGO-activists and practitioners are progressive, with left-wing sympathies and with guiding values such as solidarity, liberation, social change, human rights and justice. The approach is rights-based. Their vision is a strong state, where NGOs play a complimentary and sometimes avant-garde role in contrast to the public sector. *The principle of solidarity* is at the core of action. For a conservative approach, guiding values are charity, aid, individual assistance and relief and a belief that the role of non-state actors, such as the private and the "civil society sectors," should be central in the implementation of welfare programs. The approach is need-based. The state should only intervene when non-state Civil Society Organizations are unable to help and provide social services to the needy. *The principle of subsidiarity* is at the core of the action.

---

42. *Global Civil Society At-a-Glance*, 11.

Political  Non-political

One of the important debates surrounding NGOs is whether they should be allowed to conduct political activities or not. Globally there has been a historical shift from charity-oriented NGOs towards an emphasis on development and later on advocacy. Analyzing the power relations in society has become a major role for many NGOs as:

> (. . .)they are challenging current power-structures structures of power-holders within the private and public spheres, whose interests often are at odds with those of the citizens.[43]

On the other hand:

> (. . .) few CSOs are involved in promoting formal democratization, the promotion of human rights and the legislation of non-profits.[44]

Most NGOs' field of action is more about meeting needs than influencing public policies and redressing inequalities. In the UK the Charities Act, which regulates the functioning of NGOs, does not allow charities to have political objectives, but the new amendments proposed in 2003, open up for "human right-activities." Most scholars would also argue that CSOs have a central role when it comes to strengthening democratic values and promoting good governance. Political parties are however, strictly speaking, not part of civil society.

GONGO  Watchdog

"GONGOs" are Governmental-Organized Non-Governmental Organizations or associations closely linked to ruling elites, government, and authorities. It may be the wife of a minister who creates an "association" which would get governmental funding and access to public sector services. The association becomes part of the state or a political party in order to win over votes or get political gains. In other situations, the dividing line between the state and NGOs is not so clear. NGOs might be organizationally independent but can become completely dependent on governmental funding and policies. They will change their policies and action depending on the current "political winds and colors."

---

43. Roy, "The Transformation."
44. Roy, "The Transformation."

There is a risk in getting too close to the power-centers leading to loss of integrity. Other NGOs have more advocacy based agendas wherein they lobby and work for social reforms and watch the performance of government on central public affairs issues that might affect the poor or other sectors of society. They may also be professional organizations with the mission to defend the rights of their members and constituencies.

FIGURE 2: Religious FBOs and Secular NGOs in the MENA-region—
A Comparative Typology[45]

Aspect	Faith Based Organizations	Non-Governmental Organizations
Definition of Overall Policy/Vision Statement	In Religious terms	In Social terms
Production	Charity Oriented, relief	Development Oriented
Financing	Self funded and State	International and Private
Constituency	Exclusive, member-based	Inclusive,
Governance	Top-down	Bottom-up
Level of intervention	Individual social assistance	Structural and advocacy
Approach	Need-based	Right-based

Minority and Confessional Groups as Civil Society Organizations

Mainly in the Middle East, there is a wide range of civil society organizations, associations, NGOs, foundations and social movements which were created by religious minorities and/or confessional groups. In a country like Lebanon these groups amount to thousands in number with hundreds of thousands of members and beneficiaries. One example is the Greek Orthodox Church in Lebanon with 467 registered associations and social institutions of different categories as follows:

---

45. Gärde, *Religious FBOs*.

Faith Based Organizations

TABLE 6: The Social and Religious Institutions & Organizations of the Greek Orthodox Church in Lebanon[46]

Kind of institution/entity	Number
Orphanage	3
Elderly home	3
Hospital	1
Schools	23
Non-profit organizations & associations	46
Primary health clinics	10
Archdioceses	6
Parishes	285
Monasteries	90
Total	**467**

Other Christian faith based organizations in Egypt and Lebanon are reaching out to members and beneficiaries through social service provisions in the areas of education, health and social development and other related welfare activities.

SIZE IS IMPORTANT, PROBABLY A QUESTION OF DEATH AND LIFE

In confessional states such as Lebanon and Iraq, the size of a given community relates directly to their representation in the parliament and the government. It is not only a question of votes, but also the constitutional design and what is considered fair and just. In the case of Lebanon, the Taef-agreement of 1989, which ended the civil war of 1975–1990, stipulates a balance of power between the Muslims and Christians where 50% of all parliamentary seats are given to the different Christian representatives and the other half to Muslims.

With the shrinking number of Christians in Lebanon, and also the Sunni in relationship to the Shiites, new tensions, issues and problems are imminent. Official data still sticks to the 50/50-formula as indicated by the Lebanese constitution. It is important to understand that the Taef-agreement was written under circumstances when the Syrian regime

---

46. Ministry of Interior, Church sources. Compiled by PhD candidate, Nicolas Shehade, University of Saint Joseph, Beirut.

had total control over Lebanon and were the dividing block between Muslims and Christians. After the Hariri killing in February 2005, the configuration of Lebanese politics and civil society has changed dramatically. Politically there is now a new ruling anti-Syrian majority of mainly Sunni, Druze and Christians under the so called Hariri block. The opposition comprises Hezbollah and Amal, the two main Shiite political parties, many Christians under General Aoun and other pro-Syrian Christian and secular parties. It is still too early to see whether these new political alliances will also affect the configuration of civil society and the way social service provision is organized. Will, for instance, this lead to a new kind of inter-religious faith based organizations where both Christian and Shiite stakeholders would invest their human and financial resources?

CONCLUSION

The pattern of civil society in the MENA-region and beyond is showing signs both of growth and development in countries such as Iraq and Morocco, but also of stagnation and marginalization in Syria, Libya and Saudi Arabia. Despite the fact that foreign migrant workers, minority groups and non-Islamic populations combined represent tens of millions of people throughout the MENA-region, their participation in civil society is in some regions (such as the Gulf) marginal and fragmented with no or limited human rights. There are however positive trends of a more enabling environment in for instance Kuwait, Qatar, Bahrain and the United Arab Emirates, which may lead to an increase of Christian faith based organizations (for example) serving hundreds of thousands of Asian and African migrant workers in these countries.

It also remains to be seen if the attempted changes and reforms in the Social Association Law in Syria will benefit civil society organizations in general and in particular minority groups such as the different Oriental Christians churches and their members. In North Africa there are positive signs in Libya, which may lead to a more dynamic civil society, a more pluralistic and democratic society, and also civil and human rights for the African, Asian and Arab minority groups resident in that country. The main problem is not the lack of resources, but the freedom, gender and human capability deficit suggested by Arab scholars in the Arab Human Development Reports.

6

The Status of Non-Muslims in a Palestinian State

Bernard Sabella

THE STATUS OF NON-MUSLIMS in a future Palestinian state is a question dependent on the nature of the eventual state. The future is never dissociated from the past nor, in this case, can it occur without reference and acknowledgment of historical, legal precedents and conventions as well as the relevant UN Resolutions and inter-state accords.[1] Besides, the traditions and practices throughout centuries have become molded into communal expectations and state recognition as in religious courts and autonomy in education, charities and other institutions. The future Palestinian state, regardless of its nature, would have to continue with these traditions and practices in addition to acknowledging the group and identity definition of non-Muslim communities as they comprise an integral part of the society and state. Relationships with the Jewish state and their developments would also impact the nature of the prospective

---

1. The importance of historical and legal international precedents and commitments to religious rights in the Holy Land cannot be overstated. Since the early centuries of Christianity and the Edict of Milan of 313 AD, the consecutive rulers of the Land have issued proclamations, edicts, covenants and firmans to highlight their commitment to religious freedom. The key rulers since early Christianity were Rome, Arab Muslims, the Ottoman Empire, the British Mandate, Jordan, Israel and the Palestinian National Authority. Besides, the UN Resolutions in specific General Assembly Resolution 181 of November 29, 1947 and Resolution 194 issued on December 11, 1948 stipulated each religious and communal rights of the various communities of the Holy Land. One of the best sources for legal documents and international resolutions and commitments is *The Avalon Project at Yale Law School*, the Lillian Goldman Law Library in Memory of Sol Goldman and can be accessed on the internet at http://www.yale.edu/lawweb/avalon/avalon.htm.

Palestinian state. But equally important is the fact that Palestine and Israel make up the Holy Land claimed and shared by the three monotheistic religions. This fact would promote the likelihood that a future Palestinian state would be inclusive rather than religiously exclusive.

At present there appears to be three possible models for a potential state in the Palestinian Territories: the first is a state based on the same legal and international premises as they operate at present in the Palestinian National Authority (PNA) with its Basic Law and its international commitments, including the Basic Agreement with the Holy See.

The second is an Islamic state based strictly on the teachings of Islam, the Laws of the Qur'an and the model of the Prophet and key historical Muslim personalities. This model would be applied if Hamas, the Islamic Resistance Movement, would gain political power and would apply its covenant.

The third model is that of a unitary state comprising Israel and the Palestinian Territories. In such a remote eventuality the basic laws of both Israel and the Palestinian Territories and their legal and international commitments, together with the traditions, conventions and practices as applied to non-Muslims and non-Jews would be incorporated.

Before proceeding with discussion of the implications on non-Muslims of each of the three possible models, it is appropriate to present brief sketches of the non-Muslim communities in the Palestinian Territories as well as of the Sunni Muslim majority.

WHO ARE THE NON-MUSLIMS IN THE PALESTINIAN TERRITORIES?

Palestinian Christians are of native stock with Arabic as their mother tongue. They number within the Palestinian Territories around 50,000 but they add up to over half-a-million worldwide out of a total Palestinian population of 8 million. In Israel, Palestinian Christians are 110,000 so altogether there are 160,000 Christians or roughly one-third of the entire worldwide Christian Palestinian population. Percentage wise they represent less than 1.5% of the population in the Palestinian Territories; less than 8% of the Arab population of Israel; roughly 2% of the entire population of Israel; and slightly above 6% of the entire Palestinian population worldwide.[2]

---

2. For more in-depth analysis on Palestinian Christians, see Sabella, "Palestinian Christians."

The Status of Non-Muslims in a Palestinian State

Jews number 270,000 settlers in the Palestinian Territories found in over 150 illegal settlements and there are around 180,000 Jews living in the settlements and urban sprawl around East Jerusalem in the areas that were occupied in the June War of 1967.[3]

Samaritans live on Mount Gerizim in Nablus in the West Bank and number between 300 to 350 persons. They are descendants of a group of Israelites who broke away from mainstream Judaism over 2,200 years ago and consider Mount Gerizim the holiest ground, which is the major distinction from mainstream Judaism. There is an association with the parable of the "Good Samaritan."[4]

Sunni Muslims are the overwhelming majority of the population in the Palestinian Territories and as such in any future Palestinian or unitary state in the Holy Land, Islam will have great influence in all areas of life. This is correct even if the future state chooses not to be a religious state.[5]

---

3. Jewish Settlements in the Occupied West Bank are one of the final status issues to be eventually negotiated between Israel and the Palestinian National Authority. It is doubtful though that Israel or the Jewish settlers would agree that the Palestinian National Authority would be in a position to control the settlers or their settlements. Hence, in the context of this chapter, non-Muslims refer primarily to Christian communities and to the smaller Samaritan community that resides in Nablus in the Northern West Bank.

4. There is a parallel Samaritan community with similar numbers in Holon in Israel. While in the Palestinian Territories, Samaritans hold Palestinian citizenship; in Holon they hold Israeli citizenship. The Samaritans have a common religion, tradition and language which is Aramaic, an ancient Hebrew language spoken by Christ. Nablus is the cultural and economic center for the Samaritans. Their members attend public schools and universities there. Some of them hold public office in the Ministries of the Palestinian National Authority. Samaritans are viewed as an integral part of the city and the population of Nablus; they are accepted and their religious practices and holy sites are accepted by their Muslim neighbors and fellow citizens.

5. The relationships of Palestinian Muslims to their Christian compatriots are based religiously on the Covenant of Umar, the Muslim Caliph who in 638 AD was handed the keys of Jerusalem by Patriarch Sophranius. Two works that complement an understanding of Umar Covenant from different perspectives are: Issa, *Les Minorities Chretiennes*, 110–24; and El-Awaisi, *Umar's Assurance*. To Muslims, Jerusalem is the third holiest city after Mecca and Medina because it was designated as the first Qiblah (direction of prayer) and it was to Jerusalem that the Night Journey of the Prophet took place. See the Qur'an Surah 17:1.

A FUTURE PALESTINIAN STATE: THE PALESTINIAN NATIONAL AUTHORITY MODEL

Judging from the *Amended Basic Law* that was promulgated on March 18, 2003[6] and the practices and positions of the Palestinian National Authority (PNA) on non-Muslims since its inception in 1993 as a result of the Oslo Accords, a future Palestinian state would provide equality before the law between Muslims and non-Muslims. *Article 9* under Public Rights and Liberties states:

> Palestinians shall be equal before the law and the judiciary, without distinction based upon race, sex, color, religion, political views or disability.

Freedom of belief is also guaranteed in *Article 18*:

> Freedom of belief, worship and the performance of religious functions provided public order or public morals are not violated.

In keeping with international conventions, historical and legal precedents as well as traditions and practices, *Article 24* of the Basic Law recognizes the existence of private schools:

> Private schools and educational institutions shall comply with the curriculum approved by the National Authority and shall be subject to its supervision.

It is important to note here that most Christian communities have ran their own private schools since the middle of the nineteenth century and some even much earlier. *Article 101* recognizes the competence of Shari'ah and Religious Courts in matters of personal status:

> Matters governed by *Shari'a* law and matters of personal status shall come under the jurisdiction of Shari'a and religious courts, in accordance with the law.

Other articles of the Basic Law such as *Article 26* and *Article 27* guarantee respectively the right to participate in political life, to form and establish unions, associations, societies, clubs and ensure the freedom of audio-visual and written media including the freedom to print, publish, distribute, and transmit as well as the freedom of individuals working in the media. While both these articles apply universally, they are neverthe-

---

6. See "Amended Basic Law" and "Basic Law."

The Status of Non-Muslims in a Palestinian State

less relevant to non-Muslims because of the tendency among Palestinians to form community clubs based on religious affiliation and to print and publish materials destined to specific religious audiences.

The Basic Agreement with the Holy See

As is clear from the *Basic Agreement with the Holy See*[7] which was signed on February 15, 2000, the Palestinian Liberation Organization (PLO) acting on behalf of the Palestinian National Authority (PNA) affirms in *Article 1*:

> (...) its permanent commitment to uphold and observe the human right to freedom of religion and conscience, as stated in the Universal Declaration of Human Rights and in other international instruments relative to its application.

In *Article 3* there is a commitment to

> (...) ensure and protect in Palestinian Law the equality of human and civil rights of all citizens, including specifically, inter alia, their freedom from discrimination, individually or collectively, on the ground of religious affiliation, belief or practice.

The regime of the "Status Quo" is recognized in *Article 4*:

> The regime of the "Status Quo" will be maintained and observed in those Christian Holy Places where it applies.

Articles 5 and *6* confer on the Catholic Church rights

> to carry out, through necessary means, her functions and traditions, such as those that are spiritual, religious, moral, charitable, educational and cultural

as well as

> rights in economic, legal and fiscal matters: these rights being exercised in harmony with the rights of the Palestinian authorities in these fields.

There is also an agreement between the two sides on the issue of Jerusalem as they declare in the *Preamble* that

> an equitable solution for the issue of Jerusalem, based on international resolutions, is fundamental for a just and lasting peace in

---

7. "Basic Agreement between."

the Middle East, and that unilateral decisions and actions altering the specific character and status of Jerusalem are morally and legally unacceptable.

The Palestinian National Authority in its relations with churches and Christian communities complies with a long historical tradition that is supplemented by legal and practice precedents. It is expected that in a future Palestinian state, this compliance would continue thus ensuring freedom and autonomy of the non-Muslim communities in running their matters of religious and personal status. It is true, though, that until statehood is formally recognized and implemented Palestine cannot become a state party to international instruments. In practice, though, the PNA respects Christian religious and communal rights and protects the holy places and their autonomy. The Christian communities run their own religious courts, schools, charities and clerical institutions without interference from the PNA. Besides, a variety of public Christian religious rites and processions take place regularly across the Palestinian Territories without hindrance from the Palestinian Authority. The mayors of Bethlehem, Ramallah, Birzeit, Beit Jala, and Beit Sahour remain Christians even though in the first two instances the two towns have ceased to have a Christian majority. This is in deference to the original Christian population of these two towns and to the international Christian character of the town of Nativity. A future Palestinian state would draw on these practices and traditions in order to ensure that Palestinian Christians remain an integral part of their society.

Quota Parliamentary Seats for Christians

Palestinian Christians are guaranteed "Quota" seats in the Palestinian Legislative Council (PLC) or Parliament. The secure seats for Christian representatives (6 seats out of 132 seats—two in the Bethlehem area; two in the Jerusalem area and one each in Ramallah and Gaza) are stipulated in the Electoral Law of 2005.[8] According to *Article 95*:

> In any constituency where there are seats reserved for Christians, such seats shall be allotted to Christian candidates who obtain a greater number of votes than the remaining Christian candidates.

---

8. *Electoral Law.*

The Status of Non-Muslims in a Palestinian State

The Christian representation in the PLC is likely to continue even if there would be changes in the electoral system. This was stated publicly by President Mahmoud Abbas of the PNA upon announcing in mid-2007 the intention of changing the electoral system. Beside their presence in the PLC, Christians are found in a variety of jobs in the public sector but particularly in the diplomatic missions of the PLO abroad.[9] Not enough Christians, though, are willing to take up offers of public employment as they prefer to have their own businesses or to work for the private sector.

Christmas was made into an official national holiday; a practice that is expected to continue into a future Palestinian state. Educational curricula were modified to promote tolerance and mutual understanding across religions and Christian education or catechism was introduced as an obligatory exam subject to finishing Christian high school students.

Nevertheless, the efficiency of the governing system in a future Palestinian state and relations with non-Muslims depends on the successful and fair enforcement of law and order. To date, the failure of law and order in certain localities, the Bethlehem area in particular, has led to raised sensitivities and to feelings that only those with force or power would prevail in any dispute. This situation not only frustrates Palestinian Christians and other Palestinians who want to see a system of law in operation but leads to many Christians opting to emigrate to join family members abroad. If the authorities in a future Palestinian state cannot enforce the basic law that guarantees equality of all and if consequently due process is in a state of disarray, then serious concern would be raised on public order with possible breakdown in inter-communal relations and the perception of the state apparatus as too weak to enforce its own laws in a fair, just and quick manner.

The Foundation of Citizenry

But this futuristic system, judged overall, would be based on an equal legal and citizenry foundation: Non-Muslims are expected to be active members and participants not because they are non-Muslim but because they

---

9. Palestinian Christians are found in key diplomatic and other public positions far above their percentage in the overall population. Among the more prominent names are: Nabil Abu Rdeineh, spokesperson for the President of the National Authority; Ms. Hanan Ashrawi the spokesperson for the Palestinian Negotiating Team in Madrid in 1991; Mr. Afif Safieh, PLO representative in Washington D.C.; Mr. Shawqi Armali, PLO representative to Brussels and most recently appointed representative to the Holy See.

are citizens. The system, nevertheless, is mindful of the Islamic nature of the society and hence it acknowledges the primacy of the Shari'ah law in state legislation but does not exclude other legal inputs, precedents and commitments. There is no intention to negate the Islamic bases of governance but, at the same time these should not interfere with the introduction of an amalgam legal system that carries out justice for all citizens, irrespective of religious or other background.

Such a system would respect inter-religious differences but would not necessarily do away with frictions and sensitivities due to mixed marriages or to a change of a father's religion from Christianity to Islam, because of a divorce or other personal reasons.[10] In this case, children of the father are themselves to become Muslims because according to the religiously based and patrilineal system children follow their father.

Freedom of religion when it comes to matters of changing one's religion is only applicable one way: non-Muslims becoming Muslims but not the other way round. Adoption by non-Muslim parents of a child whose religion is unknown is not possible; again because of the stipulation that a child with unknown religion is automatically a Muslim. Certainly, there are accommodating ways and means to overcome the inconveniences of such a system but individual rights can and do suffer.

But the overall concern is not simply personal or individual as the peace between the communities is paramount and all strive not to strain inter-communal relations when sensitive personal status issues arise. Certainly, the system as found in the Palestinian Territories is not similar to what is practiced in states that apply one law to all citizens. The amalgam of laws and courts, while intended to do justice to non-Muslim communities and to insist at the same time on the primacy of Shari'ah law, make matters of family and personal status the clear domain of religious law and courts without necessarily resolving all of the disputes that are likely to emerge as a result.

---

10. Latin Patriarch of Jerusalem Monsignor Michel Sabbah has spoken in various interventions inside and outside the country of the overall Palestinian situation of continued Israeli military occupation and the need for a political solution that would guarantee peace with justice. His Beatitude is always consistent when he raises sensitive issues, such as personal status matters that are cause for disputes and that may have repercussions not simply on individuals but also on inter-communal relations. See the website of the Latin Patriarchate of Jerusalem including His Beatitude's intervention in May 2005 to the Catholic Bishops Conference of the East held in Lebanon under the title *The Church in the Holy Land: Engagement and Challenges of Christians*, originally presented in French.

The Status of Non-Muslims in a Palestinian State
Question of Identity and Equal Citizenship

But one should not be too harsh on the legal system of a future Palestinian state on the PNA model or basis. Palestinian Christians, like Muslims, use religion as a basis for group identity and for social organization. Accordingly, they would not want to do away with historical and legal rights and precedents gained as a result of religious identity and presence in the land. On the other hand, they want to be an integral part of the society as equal citizens. The incompatibility that may arise between application of religious and communal rights and prerogatives and those of citizenship should be addressed in order to minimize negative effects. The model of an altogether secular democracy would not apply in our case, even with the PNA model of a future state. While some would like for Arab Muslim society to become pluralist and democratic; pluralism and democracy have to consider the religious organizing principle of society. Certainly, the quality of pluralism and the meaning of democracy in a future Palestinian state would be impacted by the religious organizing principle. The measure of success of a pluralist democracy imprinted by religious requisites depends not simply on the efficiency of the system but on its impartiality when dealing with issues that raise concern between non-Muslims and Muslims. In their narrower interpretations and dogmatic subscription, traditional and religious precepts and prescriptions could raise sensitivities not simply on inter-religious grounds but also on social and legal rights as well. And yet these precepts are inherent in the fabric of our life in Palestinian society. Accordingly, we have to positively deal with them as comprising essential elements of a public order that is equally open to all citizens, irrespective of religious and other background characteristics. If we all, Palestinian Muslims and Christians, succeed in molding such a public order then we would have started on the process of creating a joint vision that can accommodate the overall Palestinian identity with our more particular religious and other identities.

A FUTURE PALESTINIAN STATE: THE ISLAMIC STATE MODEL

In such a state, the whole land of Palestine becomes an Islamic Waqf or Trust for perpetuity. The Covenant of the Islamic Resistance Movement

(Hamas) issued on 18 August 1988[11] declares Palestine as an Islamic Waqf:

> It, or any part of it, should not be squandered: it, or any part of it, should not be given up. Palestine is an Islamic Waqf land consecrated for Moslem generations until Judgment Day.

The Shari'ah is the source of legislation as it is God's Law and accordingly overrides earthly and human-driven laws. A perfect society is only possible through the application of religious law. Accordingly, in any future Islamic Palestinian state, the legal system would be overly imprinted with the sacred law derived from the Holy Qur'an and the Prophetic Sunnah and the traditions and examples of key Muslim personalities throughout the ages.

Muslims and non-Muslims would have to abide by the provisions of Shari'ah law and the state would become the embodiment of the Islamic Ummah. As such the equality in most rights and obligations granted to non-Muslims would be based on the acceptance by non-Muslims of this fact and their behavior accordingly. Provisions are made for all to enjoy the fruits of the land, as opposed to ownership which remains strictly Muslim. Relations with the followers of other religions are guided by Islamic tolerance. Hamas, according to *Article 31* of its convention:

> does not antagonize anyone except if it is antagonized or if they stand in its way to hamper its moves and waste its efforts.

Followers of other religions have

> the duty (...) to stop disputing the sovereignty of Islam in this region (...)

The nature of the relationships with followers of other religions depends on their behavior towards Islam and Muslims:

> Allah does not forbid you respecting those who have not made war against you on account of [your] religion, and have not driven you forth from your homes, that you show them kindness and deal with them justly; surely Allah loves the doers of justice.[12]

In particular this verse is the basis for providing equality in rights and responsibilities to Christians in Palestinian society. Palestinian Christians

---

11. *Covenant of the Islamic.*
12. *Qur'an*, 60:8.

have acted justly on the question of Palestine while Jews have not. Accordingly, relations with Christians should be based on kindness and justice, unlike relations with Jews.

A Religiously Based Government

The principle of citizenship and pluralist democracy would increasingly fade with the strengthening of the religious bases of governance. Hence, all aspects of life and not simply the religious, personal status and communal aspects would become governed by the stipulations of sacred law. A future Islamic Palestinian state would not tolerate secularism as this contradicts religious ideology. *Article 27* of the Hamas Covenant which deals with the Palestine Liberation Organization, states that:

> Secularism completely contradicts religious ideology (. . .) The Islamic nature of Palestine is part of our religion and whoever takes his religion lightly is a loser (. . .) The day the Palestine Liberation Organization adopts Islam as its way of life, we will become its soldiers, and fuel for its fire that will burn the enemies.

This particular article throws light on the insistence of some of the Hamas leadership for the movement to join the PLO on condition that the number of seats allocated to the movement would secure a majority for it since it won the parliamentary elections of January 2006. Needless to say that securing a majority of seats in the PLO would lead to the implementation of the Hamas Covenant which is the creation of a Palestinian state based on Islam and its religious ideology.

There is doubt that an Islamic Palestinian state would restrict Christian and non-Muslim communities from exercising the autonomy in religious courts, charities, schools and other communal enterprises that have become rightful privilege throughout centuries and that accrue to them because they have acted justly on the question of Palestine. The January 2006 *Electoral Platform of Hamas*[13] shows more pragmatism than the 1988 Covenant as it considers Christians equal to Muslim citizens with equal rights and responsibilities. The platform calls for a culture of dialogue and respect to all opinions that do not contradict the belief of the people and its cultural heritage. In addition, it shows also interest in Christian holy places as it calls

---

13. *Electoral Platform.*

for a national platform in order to preserve the blessed Aqsa Mosque, Jerusalem and the Muslim and Christian Holy Places.

A future Islamic Palestinian state, nevertheless, may require more stringent compliance on school curricula, the enforcement of a dress code in public, the prohibition of public expressions such as cultural performances, the mixing in public of males and females, the presentation of art and music productions that are deemed a breach to public morality and all behavior and expression that challenge or is disrespectful of religion and its key figures. One of the principal problems in implementing religious law depends on interpretation and on how behavior from Christians is perceived as in compliance with "not disputing the sovereignty of Islam" and as "acting justly" towards the question of Palestine.

Recent developments in the Gaza Strip where a chapel belonging to one of the Catholic orders of nuns was ransacked following the military takeover of Hamas of the Gaza Strip in June of 2006 and where a Christian Palestinian working for the Bible Society was killed in October 2007 point to the problematic of reining in undisciplined Muslim groups that can justify attacks on non-Muslims under any pretext but especially religious ones.[14] While the Hamas leadership was quick to deal with the inter-communal repercussions of these two incidents and emphasized once and again its condemnation to these practices, it is doubtful that those responsible will be brought to justice. At the same time, these incidents increase fear among the small Christian Palestinian community in the Gaza Strip that the future does not hold good prospects and that it is impossible for Christian Palestinians to stay put in the Gaza Strip.

---

14. The attack on the Sisters of Rosary Convent during the military confrontation between Hamas and Fatah in Gaza was condemned by Palestinian officials and also by some Hamas leaders in the Gaza Strip. It was widely reported in the international press. See an interview with the Roman Catholic priest in Gaza Monsignor Father Manuel Musallam on the incident and its repercussions in AsiaNews.it on June 19, 2007. Rami Khader Ayyad, a Palestinian Christian in Gaza, was kidnapped and later killed on October 9, 2007. All of the major political groups condemned the killing and asked for the arrest of those responsible. Rami was working for the Bible Society which was accused of proselytizing activities. It is rumored that the kidnappers had asked Rami to become a Muslim but has refused. Islam does not ask Christians, Jews and Sabians to change their religion since their religions are acknowledged in the Holy Qur'an as believing in the One God. The killing of Ayyad has raised fears among the 2,500 mostly Greek Orthodox Palestinian Christian community of Gaza. Many of them think that if such killing or kidnapping would recur then they would seriously think of leaving Gaza permanently.

The Status of Non-Muslims in a Palestinian State

Reverting to Concepts Incompatible with Equal Citizenship

There is also fear that some among the Muslim religious leadership would revert to concepts such as the Jizyah tax and the Dhimmi status[15] of non-Muslims and would want to apply them. If this were to happen, it would give Christian and non-Muslim communities a reason for grave concern, irrespective of apologetic explanations and interpretations on how the applicability of these concepts would make non-Muslims more equal citizens under the Islamic state. Applying Dhimmi status would mean that Christians and non-Muslims are protected citizens, as such they would be asked to serve the Islamic state but they cannot be fully equal because of their religious background.

The Hamas electoral platform that speaks of Christian Palestinians as equal citizens in rights and obligations could be seen as an indication that the Dhimmi status would not be applied in a future Islamic state. Palestinian Christians argue that they exist in Palestine not because they are a protected religious group but by virtue of their ancestry, long history and the fact that they are Palestinians. Accordingly non-Muslims owe their existence and continuity to no other religious group but to their history on the land that predates the arrival of Islam and to their Palestinian identity and solidarity with their own people and society. Hence, the concepts of Jizyah and Dhimmi are seen as not promoting the welfare of non-Muslims in a Palestinian society in an equitable manner but importantly the respect that Christian Palestinians show to Islam and its tolerance does not automatically make them see the advantages of an Islamic state that may not be as accommodating to their specific particularities as it is made to be.

This is particularly so if half-learned interpreters of Shari'ah law and modes of behavior that derive therefrom offer explanations or issue judgments that may be seen as prejudicial to non-Muslims. The mass of Muslim faithful would see such interpretations as binding and may lead some of them to action that may drive fear into the hearts and lives of

---

15. Jizyah is a poll tax imposed on able bodied non-Muslim men of military age. Non-Muslim citizens who pay the tax are permitted to practice their faith and to enjoy a measure of communal autonomy as well as being entitled to Muslim protection from outside aggression and being exempted from military service amongst numerous other exemptions to levies upon Muslim citizens. The term Dhimmi connotes an obligation of the state to protect the individual, including the individual's life, property, and freedom of religion and worship, in exchange for subservience and loyalty to the Muslim order and the Jizyah tax.

their fellow non-Muslims. In order not to allow for this possibility, there is need for a strong learned religious and civil leadership in a future Islamic Palestinian state. Intimidation in the name of religion can become standard in a future Islamic Palestinian state particularly if those making the intimidation are vocal and powerful. Other Muslims, though differing in interpretation, may be swayed simply out of intimidation. This is a danger of which non-Muslims are apprehensive and that may have dire consequences on inter-communal and inter-faith relations in a future Islamic Palestinian state. Hence the institution of an Islamic state in Palestine should ensure that those in charge are learned and impartial and that intimidation, under any pretext, should not be allowed or given vent.

ACKNOWLEDGING LEGAL AND RIGHT PRECEDENTS

But one essential component of any future Palestinian state, including a religiously based state, is acknowledgement of legal precedents, practices, conventions, UN resolutions and other relevant agreements and traditions that address religious and other rights of the different communities. While it is prudent to query whether an Islamic state would acknowledge any claims on the part of Christians and non-Muslims deriving from historical and religious association to the land prior to the arrival of Islam in the seventh-century, it is expected that the Islamic state, in the case that it comes into being, would not ignore the relevance of such claims to rights and practices that have been exercised for centuries. In particular, the fact that Palestine is equally Holy Land to the three monotheistic faiths is in itself a strong factor that would impact the nature of an Islamic state. Claims of religious superiority could be countered by claims of others for their own religious superiority; the danger accordingly is for the monotheist tradition to turn into a separating force rather than one of potential harmony and coming together of all citizens, irrespective of religious background.

The relevance of discussing the Covenant and the Electoral Platform of Hamas and the position on followers of other religions lies in the fact that a significant minority of Palestinians are leaning towards the establishment of a religious state. This was certainly the case in July 2007 when an opinion poll showed that 44% of Palestinians (48% in the Gaza Strip to 42% in the West Bank) wanted to establish an Islamic rule of law in the Gaza Strip. An overwhelming percentage of Hamas supporters (83%)

wished for such a development while only 20% of Fatah supporters.[16] No opinion poll was taken since then on this topic and accordingly one cannot tell whether the performance or non-performance of Hamas in the Gaza Strip since it took over power there would alter opinion on a future Islamic state. It is also important to consider that the position of Hamas with respect to Christians is based on Christian Palestinian behavior that is not aggressive against Islam and Muslims. Hence the bond is one of non-aggression rather than citizenship or acknowledgement by Hamas of particular claims of Christian Palestinians to the land and its sacred legacy and history to them. Hence Christians, like Muslims, can enjoy the same rights and obligations in Palestinian society under these conditions.

The experience of Palestinian Christians with Islam has been one of a tradition of tolerance, openness and mutual acceptance and respect. Without educating future generations of Palestinians, both Muslims and Christians, on this tradition there could be developments within a future Islamic state that would opt for narrower interpretations and for selective enforcement of laws and regulations based solely on religious grounds and power politics. This development, if it were to take place, would be seen as increasingly exclusivist and would send a message to non-Muslims that they are not on an equal footing with their Muslim compatriots. Palestinian Christians are very vulnerable to factors that push them to emigration and to join family members abroad. If a future Islamic Palestinian state turns into such a push factor, then it would be clear that this state has failed in meeting one of its essential requirements: treating Christians and Muslims as equal citizens with similar rights and obligations.

A FUTURE PALESTINIAN-ISRAELI UNITARY STATE MODEL

A future unitary state in Palestine and Israel would most likely preserve the legal precedents, conventions and agreements signed and or respected by both the Palestinian National Authority and the State of Israel. While strong religious influence would be exerted on the legislation of the state by both Jewish and Muslim groups, it is more likely that religious law would be respected, side by side, with civil law without giving religious law prevalence over legal and due processes. The practices that go back for centuries, whether they be Jewish, Christian, or Muslim would be

---

16. *Political chaos.*

acknowledged and the autonomy of religious communities in their respective clerical, educational, health, welfare and other charitable institutions would be upheld.

In Israel, the basis of all religious institutions dates back to the Ottoman Empire (1402–1921) and its system of confessional group autonomy called the millet-system.[17] Under the millet, each religious group was allowed limited independence in running its own community under a recognized (usually religious) leader who represented the community politically to the imperial authorities. Matters of law relating to personal status—marriage, divorce, inheritance, legitimacy of children—were also left to community control, so long as they did not involve a Muslim, in which case the Shari'ah (Islamic law) courts took precedence. This is not fundamentally different from the system and practice that exist in the Palestinian Territories as both Israel and the PNA recognize the Ottoman legal and communal precedents as well as those of the British Mandate (1921–1948).

A Challenging Amalgam of Laws

The amalgam of laws and the variety of legal and international instruments that should be considered in creating the legislation for the new unitary state would be a formidable task. The practical result of all these separate and semiautonomous judiciaries based on religious grounds is that, for a large area of law dealing with matters of personal status, there is no civil code or judiciary that applies to all Israeli citizens. Marriages, divorces, adoptions, wills, and inheritances are all matters for adjudication by Christian clerics, Muslim *qadis*, or *dayanim* (sing., *dayan*; Jewish religious judge). This is also applicable to the Palestinian Territories but is less problematic there since it is there a dual system of Muslim and Christian religious judiciaries and not, as in Israel, a tripartite system.

---

17. The Ottoman millet system which translates into autonomous religious, administrative and judicial arrangements for non-Muslim communities was initiated by imperial decrees knowsn as *Khatt-i-Sherif 1839* which is the first charter of liberties and guarantees to Muslim and non-Muslim which assures "to our subjects a perfect security to life, honor and fortune (. . .)" these same guarantees were confirmed in *Khatt-i-Humaioun of 1865* which granted Christian "Millets" or religious autonomous communities some internal autonomy and judicial personality under a responsible head, the Patriarch. Issa, *Les Minorities*, 61; See also Kymlicka, *Multicultural Citizenship*, 156. For a more general overview of Christians and Jews in the Ottoman Empire see Broude and Lewis, *Christians and Jews*.

An essential practical difficulty is that, in strictly legal terms, marriages across confessional lines are problematic. Another result is that citizens find themselves under the jurisdiction of religious authorities even if they are themselves secular. This situation has posed the greatest problem for the Jewish majority, not only because most Jewish Israelis are neither religiously observant nor Orthodox, but also because the hegemony of Orthodox Halakah has from time to time raised issues of fundamental concern to modern Israel. Foremost among these has been the issue of "Who is a Jew?" in the Jewish state.[18]

The essential basis for such a legal amalgam, though, would be the right of the citizen as a citizen and not as a Jew, Christian or Muslim. The counterclaims of superior religious right to the Holy Land, whether through special covenants with the Almighty or through holy books that prescribe big and small decisions on matters of life and death, economy and society, would have to reconcile to a civil legal system. Under such a system the important religious principle and belief that goes into organizing life is not excluded as a source for legislation but legislation would need to be such as to do justice to all citizens, irrespective of religious and or ethnic background.

SIMILARITY OF PALESTINIAN BASIC LAW AND ISRAELI LEGAL SYSTEM ON RELIGIOUS RIGHTS

The Basic Law of the Palestinian National Authority and the legal system in Israel both have similar structures when it comes to religious and communal rights and courts. This is corroborated by examining the *Fundamental Agreement of Israel with the Holy See* signed on December 30, 1993 and the *Basic Agreement of the PLO with the Holy See* signed on February 15, 2000. Both affirm their commitment to the Universal Declaration of Human Rights and to uphold and observe the human right to freedom of religion and conscience. The prerogatives given to the Catholic Church in running its own religious courts, schools and other related affairs are also similar and can be applied to both non-Jews and non-Muslims in Israel and the Palestinian Territories. The only exception between the two fundamental agreements lies in the *Preamble* of the Basic Agreement with the PLO whereby

---

18. For a discussion of the religious situation and its legal implications see U.S. Library of Congress Website at http://countrystudies.us/israel/45.htm.

> an equitable solution for the issue of Jerusalem, based on international resolutions, is fundamental for a just and lasting peace in the Middle East, and that unilateral decisions and actions altering the specific character and status of Jerusalem are morally and legally unacceptable.

Conclusively then, there is a common basis for practices that will cover the non-Jews and the non-Muslims in both Israel and the Palestinian Territories and this could be one of the bases for a future unitary state. Nevertheless, the power and control of the religious establishment is perceived differently in the two territories: while the infringement of the religious courts on the life of secular Israelis is resented, the majority of Israelis can still live with them if they do not infringe on the overall quality of life and individual choice. In a more religiously oriented society, such as the Palestinian Territories, the expectation is that the religious law would have to be considered not simply as applicable to personal and family matters but would cover wider areas of public order, morality and conduct. Practicalities and facts of life would most likely lead to the adoption of legislation that would incorporate existing ones and introduce new laws to satisfy the needs of a singular unitary state composed of three faiths and two nationalities.

A LAND SACRED TO THREE RELIGIONS

An elementary characteristic of such a state would be an acknowledgement of the sacredness of the land to Judaism, Christianity, and Islam without prejudice to claims of one religion over the other two. A process of accommodation needs to occur of a magnitude that would necessitate dramatic changes not simply in the legal system but in the religious, political, educational, cultural, social, economic and public spheres. In such a state, while rights are respected without reference to the background or particular characteristics of those exercising these rights, individuals and groups would feel at home in spite of their differences. Hence the challenge would be how to move from separation and retribution to unity and reconciliation. Not many people across Israel and the Palestinian Territories would think today that such a unitary state is possible, but to altogether eliminate it from the possibility of occurrence would not do justice to the three major religions and the two nationalities that co-habit the land. Some Christians would see the prospect of the development of a unitary state as most beneficial to them. By securing religious rights and subscribing to religious courts—Jewish and Muslim alike—Christians similarly would feel that they are in a more secure position as the unitary state is more likely to respect and honor their rights and not to infringe on their autonomous management of their communal and church affairs. The system of governance would be such that Christians would feel themselves to be equal citizens but the principal challenge would be whether such a unitary state can forge the elements, institutions and values that would promote equality among all of its citizens in spite of power differences and conflicting claims, religious and other, to the land and to its spiritual and material resources. Prospects for a unitary state are quite distant if not unrealistic. As a model, the unitary state can imprint on both Palestinians and Israelis the values of openness, freedom and mutual acceptance of differences within a framework of equal citizenship. All communities can live in equality and contribute to the integrity of being part of the Holy Land, its history and society while maintaining and honoring distinct religious and communal histories and traditions.

A PALESTINIAN CHRISTIAN POSITION

The two models for a future Palestinian state and the model of a unitary Palestinian-Israeli state pose different challenges and raise various expectations for non-Muslims and for those not in a position of numeric majority. But judging from the Palestinian Christian position as reflected in the *Memorandum of Heads of Churches on Jerusalem* issued in November 1994, it is clear that Christians opt for an inclusivist position in the sense that what applies to their rights also applies to the rights of Muslims and Jews:

> In claiming these rights for themselves, Christians recognize and respect similar and parallel rights of Jewish and Muslim believers and their communities. Christians declare themselves disposed to search with Jews and Muslims for a mutually respectful application of these rights and for a harmonious coexistence, in the perspective of the universal spiritual vocation of Jerusalem.[19]

Christians are concerned about the exercise of their religious rights such as freedom of worship and conscience, civil and historical rights, and rights

---

19. "Memorandum."

to have their own institutions. But these concerns do not negate their role, like other compatriots, as equal citizens according to the Memorandum:

> Local Christians, not only in their capacity as Christians per Se, but like all other citizens, religious or not, should enjoy the same fundamental rights for all: social, cultural, political and national.

Accordingly, Palestinian Christians do not see a contradiction in their dual identities as Christians and as Palestinians. As a famous saying in Arabic culture spells out: Religion is for God and the Fatherland is for everybody. This Palestinian Christian position is borne out by a history of living side by side with Muslims in what has become known as the "dialogue of life." In any future state Palestinian Christians want to ensure that they persevere and that their communities carry on their centuries-old heritage and traditions of religious, cultural, communal and social contributions without prejudice to themselves or to others. A unitary state would perhaps be the most ideal option but the least realizable at present. An a-religious, open, pluralist and democratic state that respects the equality of citizens as citizens and not due to their particular religious backgrounds most likely would be preferable to a strictly religious state. In the end, however, all of us together will build the vision for the future state: Palestinian Christians definitely have an important role in the process and they have to take up their role without any apology.

7

Managing Christian-Muslim Relations in Pakistani Setting

Mehboob Sada

ALTHOUGH PAKISTAN'S FOUNDING FATHER envisioned an enlightened Muslim state with equality among all citizens, Pakistan has been increasingly Islamized at the expense of non-Muslim minorities. There are moderate streams of Islam active within Pakistan but "Islamist" or "extreme Islam" has gained influence within the society and at the political level. This has deteriorated the situation to the extent that managing minority-majority, specifically Muslim-Christian, relations has become a delicate task.

A gradual attrition of minority rights in Pakistani law has weakened the status of non-Muslims socially, legally, and economically. Christians and other non-Muslims suffer serious inequalities in Pakistani society. Harassment of individuals is not uncommon while instances of violence against churches, other Christian organizations and communities continue to occur.

The attitude of the government, hate elements among minority and majority groups, and their representatives have further widened this gulf. The need of the time is to devise a strong strategy for developing an understanding between Christian and Muslim communities. To achieve this objective, a heartfelt and sustainable effort is needed.

CHRISTIAN-MUSLIM RELATIONS: AN OVERVIEW

Christian-Muslim relations in the Indian subcontinent, before and after partition, are marked by diverse ups and downs even though the Christian community of the area played an important role in the freedom movement against British colonial rule.

As far as the development of churches and other Christian organizations are concerned, the contact of Christian communities with the soil in modern day Pakistan can be traced back to the early twentieth century.

The Pakistan Christian Council was formed in the 1920s and links about half a million Protestants in common concerns. Its largest constituent member is the Church of Pakistan which was formed in 1970 through the union of Anglicans, United Methodists, Presbyterians of the Sialkot Church Council, and Lutherans. It has eight bishops which preside over eight dioceses covering the whole of Pakistan. These dioceses are: Karachi, Hyderabad, Lahore, Raiwind, Sialkot, Faisalabad, Peshawar, and Multan. Certain church groups including the United Presbyterians, Presbyterians of the Lahore Church Council, and the Associate Reformed Presbyterians did not wish to be included in the Pakistan Christian Council. Denominations and church groups which are currently in Pakistan are (in descending order of membership size): Roman Catholic Church, the Church of Pakistan, the Presbyterian Church of Pakistan, the Associated Reformed Church of Pakistan, Salvation Army, United Church in Pakistan, National Methodist Church, Christian Brethren, Full Gospel Assembly, Indus Christian Fellowship, Pakistan Christian Fellowship, and Evangelical Alliance Churches. In Pakistan, church and mission bodies have been working together with a renewed emphasis on laying firm foundations through emphasizing personal Christian commitment.[1]

The history of Christians in the Indian sub-continent has had a common political objective with the Indian National Congress in not supporting the idea of dividing the area while Christians of the Punjab openly sided with Muslims working for the creation of Pakistan. When Master Tara Singh, standing on the steps of the Punjab Assembly, brandished his sword and shouted "Those who want Pakistan will only get the graveyard" the then leader of Christians, S. P. Singha, supported Pakistan. Bhim Sen Sachar and Gulzari Lal Nanda of the Congress tried to put pressure on

---

1. "A short History," 3.

Managing Christian-Muslim Relations in Pakistani Setting

Christians, offering them important ministerial portfolios in India when soliciting their votes on whether Lahore should go to India or Pakistan.[2]

On 25 July 1947, Singha stated on behalf of the Christians that they should be counted along with the Muslims.[3] Actually, even during the movement for Pakistan, a union had come about between the Muslim League and the Indian Christian Association. Compared to the Congress, the Muslim League offered greater concessions to the minorities, particularly the Christians. It was on the basis of this agreement that the leaders of Indian Christians took a leading part in the Pakistan movement and showed their preference for the Muslim League against the Congress.[4]

Beginning with the early days of the creation of Pakistan and before the partition of the Indian subcontinent, there were a number of minorities in Pakistan, the Sikhs and the Christians being the most important. The situation of Sikhs was much more complicated because like Muslims, they were also asking for a separate homeland. Actually, the entire dispute was related to the Punjab. Hindus, Sikhs, Parsees, and other minorities of Sindh, the Frontier and Balochistan had already thrown their lot and their future with Pakistan.[5]

The role of the Christian community in the political struggle, socio-economic efforts for nation building, and their relations with the Muslim community were always significant. The political struggle for the attainment of a separate homeland for Muslims was not just confined to the Muslims but was supported, directly or indirectly, by the Christian community.

For centuries, Christians and Muslims have shared this land in peace and harmony. During the last decades, there were incidents and events that severely effected their relations such as the separate electorate system, blasphemy laws, and other extra-judicial and discriminatory policies that were based on socio-political biases, hatred, maltreatment of poor working classes, targeting and destruction of sacred and holy places of Christians, and blaming their religious belief systems.

---

2. Parshad, "Pak-o-Hind."
3. Zia, "Tehreek-e-Pakistan," 36.
4. Nadeem, *Yeh Des Hamara*, 60.
5. Salim et al., *Violence, Memories*, 90.

CHANGING FACE OF CHRISTIAN-MUSLIM RELATIONS IN THE PRESENT TIME

Since September 11th 2001, Christian-Muslim relations in Pakistan have gone through fundamental transformations. The measures taken by Musharraf's government to curb Islamic militancy in the country have brought a sigh of relief from the majority of the people including Christians. From the government of Zia-ul-Haq to Pervez Musharraf's regime, moderate Muslims and religious minorities in the country who support inter-faith dialogue, have felt threatened by the growing power of Muslim extremism and ensuing intolerance.

The ice seems to be melting now as another positive development, the abolition of a sixteen-year old system of separate electorate for Pakistan's religious minorities, has occurred. Religious minorities have long claimed that the separate electorate introduced by General Zia-ul-Haq in 1985 marginalized them from mainstream politics. According to this system, religious minorities could only vote for candidates of their own community to get a few reserved seats in the Provincial and National Assemblies. They could not vote for Muslim candidates in the general elections. The system based on the Islamic concept of "Dhimmis" (second class citizens) segregated and discriminated against religious minorities by cutting them off from the mainstream national political life. The churches, Christians and progressive Muslim organisations like the Human Rights Commission of Pakistan waged a long struggle against this system of "electoral apartheid."

The Christian community welcomed the decision to restore joint elections and all religious minorities welcomed the decision made by the Sindh High Court reiterating that the constitution did not bar a non-Muslim from serving in the high court and denying a petition to remove Justice Rana Bhagwandas from the bench for being a Hindu. These positive steps encouraged and built the confidence of minority communities that were frightened by the prospect of "Talibanization" of society in Pakistan. Such actions, though few and far between, did pave the way to peace and negotiation.

Another significant development is the desire of some Muslim religious groups and organizations to have inter-religious dialogues and joint events to promote peace and harmony. Christian-Muslim seminars and inter-religious prayer services are being organized in all major cities to promote peace in the region.

CHRISTIAN CONTRIBUTIONS TO PAKISTANI SOCIETY

Christian communities have always played a vital role in all aspects of nation building, especially in the areas of education, health and social welfare. Unfortunately, this commendable role of Christian communities has never been appreciated or mentioned in historical accounts in Pakistan.

> Our recorded history is not the history of the collective flow of life. Instead it records the exploits of rulers, political intellectuals and minions of governments and despotic overlords. Quite naturally, this pattern of Pakistan's history ignores the significant role played by ethnic or religious minorities. In fact, during the freedom movement of the subcontinent, had the political leader not proved to the colonial power that the masses including minorities were with them, Pakistan could have not been achieved.[6]

On the other hand, historical evidence gives thought provoking facts about the role of the Christian community that are undoubtedly noteworthy. Despite their exceptional contributions in the fields of education, health, politics, trade, and industry, it is depressing to note that Christian-Muslims relations are still marred by misinformation in Pakistan. A short review is given below to make it apparent that these contributions are by no means inferior to that of the majority communities in Pakistan.[7] Christian missionaries have, no doubt, helped in setting a high standard of education in the country and have played an equally commendable role in the health care sector. Quaid-i-Azam Mohammad Ali Jinnah had assured equal rights and opportunities to the minority communities of Pakistan.

> Many educationists from the Christian community contributed tremendously in the development of the motherland. Michael M. R. Chohan, Principle St. Patrick College Karachi is one of them.[8]

---

6. Salim et al., *Violence, Memories*, 20.
7. Salim, *Role of Minorities*, 185.
8. Interview with Hameed Henry.

Christian missionary educational institutions play an important role in imparting quality education to people, and it must be noted that the current top leadership of the country was educated at missionary institutions.[9]

As well, Christians have made immense contributions to other areas of Pakistani national life. Pakistan's first non-Muslim and certainly the most respected Chief Justice of Pakistan Supreme Court was Justice A.R. Cornelius who served in this capacity from 1960 until 1968. Pakistani Christians also distinguished themselves as great fighter pilots in the Pakistan Air Force, notable among them are Cecil Chaudhry, Peter O'Reilly and Mervyn L. Middlecoat. Christians distinguished themselves as educationists, doctors, lawyers, businessmen and athletes. One of Pakistan's greatest batsmen, Yousuf Youhana, was Christian but converted to Islam, changing his name to Mohammad Yousuf.

Law-makers, judges and lawyers from minority communities did all that was humanly possible to raise the prestige and honor of the judicial system. The history-making decisions of Justice A. R. Cornelius and Justice Dorab Patel, two judges of the highest integrity, have added brilliance to the reputation of the judiciary in Pakistan and have enabled it to hold itself in well-deserved self-esteem.[10]

In addition to the struggle for upholding the law, Christian lawyers played a prominent role at the social and political levels. At present, there are hundreds of Christians in the police of the Punjab, Sindh, and Balochistan. After independence, many Christians joined Pakistan Railways and did well in that department.

In the terrible situation that prevailed during the 1971 war in the then East Pakistan, Christian soldiers such as Colonel Javed Jalal, Major Justin Sharf, Lieutenant General Julian Peter, Major Richard, and Second Lieutenant David Atarad stood resolutely facing the Indian army. The first four were made prisoners-of-war and remained in Indian captivity for two and a half years while Lieutenant David Atarad lost his life. On the medical side, Colonel Parveen of nursing services and Colonel Catherine Mark tended the sick and the wounded in extremely trying circumstances. The former received the *Sitara-e-Imtiaz*, "the star of excellence," for her services.[11]

9. Rao, "Religious harmony."

10. Interview with Rana Qaaiser Iqbal, Advocate, President, Amnesty International Pakistan.

11. Salim, *Role of Minorities*, 362.

Managing Christian-Muslim Relations in Pakistani Setting

Another important area is the health sector. Christians in Pakistan, as in other fields of life, helped to provide facilities of treatment and medical care to all people without thought to their religious affiliation. Their role in making available health and medical aid in rural areas and backward regions, both before the partition and afterwards, has been particularly outstanding. A key leadership role was played in this sphere by Christian missions and church organizations. Hospitals and health centers established by the Christian community still serve the people of Pakistan in all four provinces. Even today, the hospitals managed by the minorities have the distinction of being the best-served and best-equipped in the country. Many of them have also received national awards for their exceptional services.

Ironically, a sizeable portion of minorities in Pakistan do not get the opportunity to benefit from the education system that their communities have created or to participate in government services. A lack of educational opportunities, poverty, the covert discrimination to which minorities are subjected, and the prevailing prejudices mean minority citizens do not rise above the menial ranks of peons and sanitary workers. Despite this constricting atmosphere, many individuals through sheer hard work and determination manage to reach high positions rendering distinguished service to their country.

During the past three decades, awareness-raising movements in minority communities have done much to give people self-confidence and encouragement, and now more and more persons have become visible in government departments. There is, therefore, a distinct improvement in minority representation in various services but as stated above, during the last sixty years their role in the services has been confined to the lowly posts of peons, sanitary-workers, ward boys in hospitals, and paramedical staff or at best, subordinate clerks.[12]

The Christian community of Pakistan has provided invaluable services in the cultural sphere. Fields like literature print/electronic media, audio-visual arts, show business and sports are living examples of their role in social life and in the cultural development of Pakistan. Before the inception of Pakistan, numerous Christians, Parsis, Hindus, Sikhs, Bahais, and Buddhists were engaged in the profession of journalism in the areas that now constitute this country. Writers from the minorities in Pakistan

---

12. Interview with Rana Qaiser Iqbal, Advocate, President, Amnesty International Pakistan.

have been active in writing poetry, drama, and prose. In the world of film, television, radio, and theatre numerous non-Muslims have made a name for themselves. The sportsmen from the minorities have marched shoulder to shoulder with their majority compatriots in making Pakistan known internationally for its proficiency in international competition.[13]

> The Christians have continued their interest and involvement in literature, and numerous Christian writers have featured in the forefront in this regard, though because of the typical social, political, economic conditions of Pakistan and the influence of extremist religious elements, they did not receive the acknowledgement they deserved. Take Nasreen Anjum Bhatti and Nazir Qaiser, for example. All well-known poets and writers of today have praised them for their sensitivity and realism in Urdu and Punjabi languages. Similarly Gulzar Wafa Chaudhry has made a name for himself in Urdu literature, and his sketches of personalities have received exceptional praise. Afzaal Firdaus is counted among the country's first rank poets for his ghazals and nazms.[14]

SUFFERINGS AND STRUGGLES OF PAKISTANI CHRISTIANS

The story of sufferings and struggles for their basic human rights under severe Islamic religious domination and the miseries of minorities in Pakistan are enormous and visible everywhere and at every level of the society. The story of the Christian community in Pakistan starts with the creation of Pakistan. Even though the founder of the nation had said on August 11, 1947, that "religion has nothing to do with State Affairs," we see that the religion of Islam has a dominating status in the constitutionalized political, judicial, social, cultural, and governmental systems. Islam is the official state religion, Shari'ah has been enforced as the supreme law of the land, and the judiciary; legislature and executive are also working under the constitutionalized law. All laws are being modified and reframed according to the injunctions of the Qur'an.

The Myth of First Class Citizen

The present constitution, political system, and government are undemocratic since theocracy prevails in different garbs, capitalizing on the

---

13. Salim, "Minorities of Pakistan," 27.
14. Ibid., 28.

Managing Christian-Muslim Relations in Pakistani Setting

foundations of the concept of 'one nation'. In this system, the Christians and other minorities have neither achieved equal politico-socio-economic status nor do they enjoy equal access to available opportunities in nation building.

Though the Christian community has always considered themselves to be equal citizens of Pakistan, the present political system and its unjustified policies never endorsed their rights. Unfortunately, the Christian community that played a significant role in the creation of Pakistan and has made admirable contributions ever since, has been reduced to second class citizens and maybe even lower. If we glance through the history of the subcontinent, the often overlooked reality is that Christians have been in existence since the first century while Islam came much later. This establishes Christian communities as pioneers in this part of the world.

Illegal Occupation and Forced Evictions

Both Christians and Muslims have been living in Pakistan peacefully for the past many decades but there are some instances that have flamed a sense of hatred creating disparities in Muslim-Christian relations. Foremost among them are the cases of illegal occupations and forced evictions. An example follows:

> Sajid Butt, a Naib Nazim of belonging to the Muslim community, demolished two Marlas godown owned by Karamat Masih, a Christian, on February 9, 2005, at Narand Mandi District Sheikupura. On Karamat's refusal Sajid Butt threatened him of dire consequences but Karamat got stay order from the court. However, the accused bulldozed the godown. No redress was provided to the affectee by the concerned authorities till report.[15]

Blasphemy and other Discriminatory Legislation

Brutal killings of innocent people and the targeting and demolishing of their places of worship are not a new phenomenon for the minorities in Pakistan. Religious leaders of Christian churches condemned massive attacks and demanded a high-level judicial inquiry and exemplary punishment to all the culprits responsible for this deliberate outrage yet very little has been done in this regard.

---

15. "A Report on" 2002–2003.

Adopted in 1986, Pakistan's *Blasphemy law* imposes life imprisonment on anyone insulting the Qur'an, and death penalty on anyone defiling the name of Prophet Mohammed. Minority and human rights activists have repeatedly called for the repeal this law as often it is used to settle private matters between individuals. So far hundreds of Christians have died because of this law. Since 1986, more than 4,000 people have been accused of blasphemy; some 560 people have been charged and 30 are still waiting for a court decision. The accused, when acquitted, have often had to relocate to save their lives and to protect their families.[16]

Bonded Labor and Illegal Detention

With reference to labor rights, it is shocking to know that in general laborers are maltreated. The existing regulations regarding labor and work lack the safeguards provisioned by law and there are serious faults in implementation of these policies.

A petition was filed by Iqbal Masih against Mehar Muhammad Ashfaq, a kiln owner who had detained thirty four workers for six months, forcing them to work. Later the detainees, including three elderly persons, ten women and fourteen kids were recovered through a *Habeas Corpus* writ.[17]

Along with this use of force, sexual harassment is also faced by kiln workers. An International Labor Organization (ILO) report on human rights conditions in Pakistan stated that women were the worst sufferers in facing sexual abuse as bonded labor.[18]

Biases of the Majority Group and the Hate Elements

There are thousands of cases registered against minority groups including Christians that are due to biased approaches and the hateful attitudes of the majority communities. The people who suffer it the most are Christians in low wage jobs such as sanitation workers, plumbers, sweepers and unskilled laborers. It is reported that such biases and resulting inhumanities are common among Muslim masses in Pakistan.

These biases against under-privileged Christians are rampant at the governmental level as well as where they are not given their rightful place.

16. "Blasphemy Law."
17. Daily The News, October 12, 2005.
18. Daily Dawn, May 21, 2005.

Managing Christian-Muslim Relations in Pakistani Setting

Our research reveals that Christian workers of almost all departments of federal and provincial governments face a number of injustices. Two are cited here: (a) The employees are not regularized but are forced to work as temporary labor for years, and (b) Their pay books and pension books were not handed over to them. In addition, Health, Municipality, and Cantonment Board administrations infringe upon worker rights and violate labor laws when the laborers have to pay bribes to the clerks to have their service records produced.[19]

Amid this, low-wage employees and workers face violence from their employers especially in domestic situations and with private companies.

Among Christians living in Pakistani villages, few are farmers or owners of land. Most are poor and have to migrate to the cities where, as Christians, they can usually only be hired as sweepers, considered to be one of the most degrading professions. This job further costs them as they are then deemed to be untouchables by Muslims and are deprived of good education, respect in society, a secure job, and a chance at a better future.

This state of affairs was observed among Christians and lower caste Hindus, mainly because their social and economic backwardness, insufficient education and persistent poverty make them easy targets for discrimination.[20] Those who are able to achieve a higher status or 'respectable' jobs enjoy a slightly more peaceful life but such individuals that go on to higher levels of public service can be counted on fingers.

Though Christian missionaries and churches ran ninety percent of educational institutions, they were disenfranchised when their institutions were nationalized by the government of Pakistan. Now the Christian community cannot benefit from education because of the policies and high expenses of these schools. At present, only 1% Christian students are receiving education from missionary and church-based schools. In fact, the only way to build a better future for this community is accessibility to education at least up to high school. This could help people to fight with dignity against all sorts of immoral discrimination and prejudices.

In short, we have entered the twenty-first century but in terms of Christian-Muslim relations in Pakistan it has still not been possible for us to build a civil society commensurate with its ideals. In our view, a lack of national priorities, under-privilege, poverty, unemployment, il-

19. "A Report on" 2002–2003, 107.

20. Interview with Razia Joseph, director of Women Shelter, Bishop's House, Faisalabad.

literacy, social injustices, and anti-people policies of successive regimes have brought the country to this sorry stage. On top of all this, political leaders bolstered by the civil and military bureaucracy and motivated by greed and power, have shamelessly exploited the noble name of Islam and Islamic justice to let the society drift into an undemocratic and corrupt environment.

DIALOGUE: THE ROAD TO HARMONY BETWEEN MUSLIMS AND CHRISTIANS

There is need for Christians and Muslims to develop lines of communication with each other for better understanding of each other's situations and problems in order to seek healthy solutions. Even when they have been living together for many years, perhaps centuries, real knowledge and appreciation of each other has often been slight. An effort to manage strong and lasting trust between Muslims and Christians must be made; otherwise, the calm that has been taken for granted may suddenly break. A harmonious environment can only be achieved through taking concrete confidence building measures such as to generate dialogue and discussions at different levels of the society and between the communities.

Both the leadership of Christians and Muslims and their masses have seen bitter conflicts provoked in recent years in different places that have in the past been noted for peaceful coexistence and mutual trust. Now, inter-religious harmony has become an illusion. Outside influences have often aggravated growing tensions since the existing bonds have not been strong enough to sustain such pressures. External involvements with their own agendas have further ruptured the social fabric of our society.

Both Christianity and Islam teach lessons of equality, justice, peace, harmony, and peaceful coexistence. It would not be difficult for religious leaders to take some responsibility for peace-building by boosting their efforts to harmonize differences and to strengthen commonalities by rejecting the policies of prejudice for each other's religion. Following are some key areas where effort needs to be made to pave the way for dialogue:

- Muslim and Christian communities in Pakistan must promote common themes in inter/intra-faith activities

Managing Christian-Muslim Relations in Pakistani Setting

- Peace and developmental efforts carried out by Muslim and Christian peace builders in Pakistan and other parts of the world must be studied for guidance and experiential learning
- Constructive methods of conflict resolution between Muslims and Christians must be based on the integration of universal and local perspectives

These efforts can only bear fruit if the clergy on both sides agree to this agenda and are able to meet regularly for discussions. The problems of this world such as drought, disease, poverty, and the displacement of persons do not acknowledge religious divisions. People of all religions including Christians and Muslims are equally effected by such calamities and so their cooperation in this struggle for betterment can yield heartening results. Joint action is important as it also proves that Muslims and Christians are not yearning for self-aggrandizement or that they are not profiting by capitalizing on people's weaknesses, instead they are truly serving their fellow humans, brothers and sisters.

The Muslims of the majority communities must be mindful when scrutinizing our own positions. We must recognize our role in inter-faith relations, debates and discussions. There needs to be identification of factors regarding the acceptance within the fold of those who do not accept us; to tolerate the intolerant; and, to identify a positive leadership. Identifying the leaders and learning from their discourses is important for the reconstruction of the discourse. For example, when dialogue is mentioned a formal discussion between experts comes to mind. It must be stated clearly that this is not the only form of dialogue needed here though this format also is important as it facilitates the dialogue about life and deeds by clarifying ideas and dissipating prejudices.

PROBLEMS AND PROSPECTS OF INTER-FAITH DIALOGUE AND HARMONY

It may be noted that much of the formal dialogue concentrates on social issues. It may be useful to examine different religious perspectives as well in order to build mutual confidence. It is understandable that it will be hard to find agreement in theological matters but inter-religious dialogue may differ from the ecumenical dialogue among Christians that aims at bringing about a unity of faith. It is obvious that Christians and Muslims will continue to differ on essential matters of faith. For this reason, the purpose of theological dialogue will not be to prove that one side is right and the other wrong but to explore respective positions in order to understand them better. When this is done many prejudices built upon half-truths will fall by the wayside.

The threat of retaliation from the existing political culture is colossal as someone speaking out against it may be jailed or silenced by other means. But the dialogue for harmony must be free from any political pressure and must be able to afford freedom of expression to participants.

Next, there are issues regarding tools and how we go about making change? There is an urgent need to develop manuals and materials for dissemination to raise awareness about minority communities and their beliefs. Later, hopefully, we can translate the ethics, tools, and topics of intra-faith dialogue into practicality. The only threat to these endeavors may come from a lack of leadership where no person is in charge—the Muslim community is large and diverse—and leadership is exercised at all levels. It is frightening to give all authority to the imams and "preachers" in leading inter-faith dialogue.

Since delicate issues are involved, it will be useful to have this activity led by groups with specialized knowledge and peace-building arguments to allow a sense of trust and authenticity. The dialogue of religious experience is sometimes merely an instance of the dialogue of discourse, distinguished by the fact that the matters under examination are the spiritual traditions of Christianity and Islam respectively. Attention may be paid to the spiritual message of the Bible and of the Qur'an, but also to the writings of spiritual authors, of Sufis and mystics. Such exchanges, especially when they take place in an atmosphere of faith in humanity, can be of immense help in generating mutual respect.

There are times also when Muslims and Christians may want to offer joint supplication to God. During the Gulf War, Christians, Muslims, and Jews came together to pray for peace.

There is no doubt that the road to dialogue and harmony in Pakistan is a difficult path to walk but this journey must be undertaken with trust and confidence that we can achieve equality and peace. Dialogue can contribute to peace by providing an understanding between individuals and communities to make them strong enough to resist outside influences. Similarly, a dialogue with a common response to the effects of war will reinforce the will to ban armed conflict as a way of resolving disputes.

Dialogue among experts will help to clarify issues and also to plan strategies. Dialogue over religious experience will help to provide motivation and will also be a source of strength to persevere.

All this may seem idealistic; nevertheless, we have to nurture the dream of attaining peace and harmony among the people in Pakistan.

Dialogue as conversation between different religions or civilizations is a need of the time. Dialogue between civilizations, often alluding to the dialogue between religions, is aimed to remove barriers and increase the amount of good in the world by a free exchange of ideas. Exclusivism, inclusivism, parallelism and pluralism are referred as dialogical attitudes but only pluralism is appropriate for successful dialogue. Islam, as a pluralistic religion, considers dialogue legitimate but both Muslims and Christians have not effectively participated in addressing different problems like extremism, mistrust, misconceptions, weaknesses, lack of proper representation, and unjust authority. These problems can be addressed within a framework that comprises tolerance, respect, sincere preparedness and loyalty to humanity as the success of inter-faith dialogue depends much on its agenda.

An agreement must be reached among participants on common points of the agenda such as universal truth, trans-cultural values and spiritual satisfaction in order to achieve the goals for which inter-faith dialogue is initiated.

On the surface, the initiatives and developments of inter-religious cooperation seem encouraging. These initiatives therefore are an attempt to show to the world that Pakistan is an open society that accepts diversity and believes in pluralism. Be that as it may, most church leaders have welcomed this new opportunity and are joining hands with the majority community in order to build a healthy relationship in peace and inter-faith harmony.

8

Non-Muslim Women in Pakistan
Minority within Minority

Yasmin Haider

In the name of God, the God of all the Prophets, the God of all the books, and the God of Day of Judgment!

ONE OF THE ASPECTS of discussing the broad topic of conceiving and evaluating the situation of non-Muslims living as minority in the Muslim states has been allotted to me under the title "The position of the Minority within Minority in Pakistan." I do not claim to do justice to the topic but can assure you that I put forward my full efforts and abilities.

Before dilating upon the issue, the topic needs analysis. The word *minority*, appearing twice in the topic, is not simply words but are contextual terms embodying different meanings.

The first use of "minority" refers to women not as a statistical "minority" but as an oppressed and weak section of society which is derived from the definition adopted on January 8, 1950 by a sub-committee appointed by the United Nations Human Rights Commission. According to said definition, the term minority includes only those non-dominant groups in a population which possess and wish to preserve stable ethnic, religious or linguistic traditions or characteristics markedly different from the rest of the population.[1] For this definition, the Muslims ruling in India, the British in India, and the whites ruling in Africa, although

---

1. Mishra and Kumar Singh, *Status of Minorities*, 121.

statistically lesser in number are the dominant power and do not fall within the definition of minority.

The second use of "minority" has a popular, general reference to religious minorities excluding the ethnic groups.

The study of the history reveals that women have always been victims and vulnerable creatures in the patriarchal society. Even the birth of a female child led the father and the family to feel shame. In the pre-Islamic period some tribes had the custom of female infanticide, i.e. killing their juvenile girls to save their honour. Though such "Honour killing" is now almost non-existent in society, it is however in practice in various alternatives like cursing her, ignoring her, preferring brother over her, and a bond of mistrust. The patriarchal attitude of society cursed and oppressed the female in all her positions. As a daughter, she is the property of her father, as a sister she is accountable to her brothers, and as wife she is subservient to her husband. In all her positions she is a disadvantaged segment of society. But unluckily, if she is a minority, she is doubly disadvantaged. Her rights are further limited and discarded for being a non-Muslim.

Before I dilate upon the position of women in Pakistan I would like to give a very brief account of the salient features of Pakistani society in which this oppressed section of the society survives. The main features of Pakistani society are the following:

1. Pakistani society is a *multicultural society* inhabited by people of different cultures like Punjabis, Pathans, Baluchis, Kashmiris, Sindhi, and Muhajirs (the migrants from India at the time of partition of the subcontinent in 1947 and their descendants).

2. Pakistan is also a *multi-faith society* having people belonging to different faiths. The total population of Pakistan is about 150 million, out of which 3.1% are religious minorities.

The main religious minorities are:[2]

1. Christians
2. Hindus
3. Bahais
4. Parsis
5. Ahmadis (legal minority)

2. *Census of Pakistan.*

Jews are not found in Pakistan or they are at least out of the demographic scene.

On the socio-economic graph, the position of Christians and Hindus is very low while the Ahmadis, Parsis and Bahais enjoy better economic positions. According to the 1998 census, the literacy rate among the Christians was 34% as compared to national literacy rate of 46.56%. Among minority women the literacy rate is very low and rather hopeless.

LEGAL ASPECTS

The Constitution of Islamic Republic of Pakistan from 1973 discriminates the non-Muslim woman as being non-Muslim. As per *Article 41* of the constitution, the president of Pakistan must be a Muslim. Even the oath of the Prime Minister and the Chief Justice of Pakistan and some other key positions requires indirectly, according to *Article 91*, that they should be Muslims. Insight pertaining to such a provision was recently demonstrated at the oath taking of the Chief Justice of Pakistan. A petition was filed in the Supreme Court by some Muslims stating that since Rana Bhagwan Das is a Hindu, a non-Muslim, he cannot become the Chief Justice of Pakistan.

In the legal framework of Pakistan a person belonging to a minority within a minority is condemned twice as a female as well as a non-Muslim. She is excluded from the mainstream of society along with the male followers of her faith and further excluded as a female within her own minority faith stream.

In Pakistan, even against Islamic doctrine, the Hudood laws have almost been made equally applicable to males and females as well as to non-Muslims and Muslims. But concerning the right of "evidence" non-Muslims as well as women have not been considered trustworthy or reliable witnesses. The Offence of Zina (Enforcement of Hudood) Ordinance 1979 provides in *Section 8*:

> (b) at least four Muslim adult male witness, about whom the Court is satisfied having regard to the requirements of tazkiyah al-shuhood that they are truthful persons and abstain from major sins (kabair) give evidence as eye-witnesses of the act of penetration necessary to the offence:

Non-Muslim Women in Pakistan

Provided that, if the accused is a non-Muslim, the eye-witnesses may be non-Muslims.[3]

Here the first word *Muslim* excludes a non-Muslim woman qua non-Muslim and the word male further excludes her as being female.

The Offences Against property (Enforcement of Hudood) Ordinance 1979 comes up with the same conditions in *Section 7*:

> (b) at least two Muslim adult male witnesses, other than the victim of the theft, about whom the Court is satisfied, having regard to the requirements of "tazkiyah-al-shuhood," that they are truthful persons and abstain from major sins (kabair), give evidence as eye-witnesses of the occurrence:
>
> Provided that, if the accused is a non-Muslim, the eye-witnesses may be non-Muslim: (...)[4]

The Prohibition (Enforcement of Hadd) Order 1979 requires at least two Muslim adult male witnesses to prove the case as Hadd, According to *Section 9*:

> (b) at least two Muslim adult male witnesses, about whom the Court is satisfied, having regard to the requirement of "tazkiyah al-shuhood," that they are truthful persons and abstain from major sins (kabair) give evidence of the accused having committed the offence of drinking liable to hadd.[5]

Also, *Section 6* of the Offence of Qazf (Enforcement of Hadd) Ordinance 1979 should be mentioned:

> (c) at least two *Muslim* adult male witnesses, other than the victim of the qazf, about whom the Court is satisfied, having regard to the requirements of tazkiyah al-shuhood that they are truthful persons and abstain from major sins (Kabair), give direct evidence of the commission of qazf:
>
> Provided that, if the accused in a non-Muslim, the witnesses may be non-Muslims.[6]

---

3. *Offence of Zina.*
4. *Offences Against Property.*
5. *Prohibition.*
6. *Offence of Qazf.*

In addition to the conditions and competence of witnesses under Hudood laws or special laws, the law of Evidence (the Qanun-e-Shahadat Order, 1984) while laying down the conditions of competence and number of witnesses in general cases makes two special provisions which exclude non-Muslims and women from the main stream. Reference is made to *Article 3* about who may testify as well as in *Article 17* about competence and number of witnesses:

> (...) Provided further that the Court shall determine the competence of a witness in accordance with the qualifications prescribed by the injunctions of Islam *as laid down in the Holy Qur'an and Sunnah* for a witness, and, where such witness is not forthcoming, the Court may take the evidence of a witness who may be available. (...)
>
> (a) in matters pertaining to financial or future obligations, if reduced to writing, the instrument shall be attested by two men or one man and two women, so that one may remind the other, if necessary, and evidence shall be led accordingly; and
>
> (b) in all other matters, the Court may accept, or act on the testimony of one man or one woman or such other evidence as the circumstances of the case may warrant.[7]

A "DOUBLE BLOW" FOR NON-MUSLIM WOMEN

Chapter XVI of Pakistan Penal Code 1860 relating to "Offences Affecting The Human Body" was totally redesigned and substituted with the so-called Islamic law of Qisas-o-Diyat.

It is to be noted that *Article 17* of the Qanun-e-Shahadat, 1984, as referred to above, provides for Islamic law of evidence by which the testimony of non-Muslims as well as of women is not accepted in Qisas. This rule is derived from tradition/Sunnah:

> The evidence of the women shall not be accepted in the cases of Hudood and Qisas.[8]

It is to be noted that the said order of the Holy Prophet in respect of evidence from women was contextual. At that time a woman was too

---

7. *Qanun-e-Shahadat*.
8. *All-Pakistan legal*, 120.

Non-Muslim Women in Pakistan

dependent and weak to give truthful evidence without fear and pressure. The bar was being dependent and weak and not being a woman.

Hence, for non-Muslim women the law provides a 'double blow': one for being non-Muslim and the other for being a woman. Hence the minority within minority are disadvantaged and disempowered doubly leaving no hope or scope of equal rights as Pakistani citizens.

The minority within minority is not only condemned in the lawbooks of Pakistan but is convicted, condemned, and harassed, sometimes as accused and sometimes as victims in criminal cases.

The report of the National Commission on Justice and Peace has provided the details of thirty-five Muslims who were accused of blasphemy, six of whom were women. The commission has also provided the details of incidents of human rights violations in respect of minority women in its 2007 report. Here are details of a few of these events.

Concerning conversions: In 1994 Ms. Carol, a seventh grade Christian girl was alleged of committing blasphemy in Sukhar. She converted to Islam in order to save herself from litigation and other possible sufferings. A similar case is that of Ms. Lakshami from the district Swabi NWFP, who was reported to have converted to Islam in jail. When the then Chief Justice of the Peshawar High Court (N.W.F.P) was visiting the jail, the Chief Judge praised her for converting to Islam. In a number of cases, minority women (Christian, Hindu, and Sikh), including minors who were abducted and converted to Islam through marriage to a Muslim. Contact with their families is made impossible on account of their conversion. The lower courts have generally ignored the circumstances (like detachment from family, the crime involved, and the age of the so called convert) and the need for enabling conditions for free consent.[9]

Concerning abductions: a Hindu girl Pampi Mai (13), daughter of Mangala Ram from Chak, Bahawalpur was abducted by a Muslim family on June 27, 2006. Misari Ludhani, a Hindu father, registered a case that his daughter Neelam Ludhani had been abducted. When the matter came into the Supreme Court, the abducted girl stated that she had embraced Islam and married Amjad of Sukkar out of her free will. The father of the abducted girl stated that he had no objection on her conversion if it was done by her free will, but he was worried about her future.[10] The Supreme

---

9. "A report on" 2007, 31–32.
10. "A report on" 2007, 33.

Court exercising its parental jurisdiction ordered that the groom's father should deposit 15 lakh as a bank guarantee, a house, and a share of Amjad's business should also be transferred to Neelam for her future security. She was permitted by the court to live with her husband and meet with her parents in the presence of her husband and father in-law.[11]

As per a report of the All Pakistan Minority Alliance (APMA), twenty-five Hindu girls were forced to convert to Islam in Sindh. Ms. Maria Samar John was abducted and married to Ghaffar when she was 17 years old. He forcibly converted her to Islam and beat her for refusing to say the Muslim prayers. She was locked in the house and abused by her husband and his family. She escaped with her infant son and was granted a divorce.

A case was registered against Nusrat Jahan, an Ahmadi woman, under blasphemy law for writing an article in a magazine.[12]

MINORITY (WOMEN) IN THE MINORITY (NON-MUSLIMS) SITUATION

It is very important to note that the personal laws pertaining to minorities as protected, date from the united India, before the creation of Pakistan, such as: The Succession Act 1925; The Christian Marriage Act 1872; The Births, Deaths and Marriages Registration Act 1886; The Divorce Act 1869; Indian (Non-Domiciled parties) Divorce Rules 1927; The Parsi Marriage and Divorce Act 1936; The Hindu Widows Marriage Act 1856; The Hindu Marriage Disabilities Removal Act 1946; The Hindu Married Womans Rights to separate Residence and Maintenance Act 1946; The Anand Marriage Act 1909; Buddhist Law 1909; and, The Arya Marriage Validation Act 1937.

The interesting and rather alarming aspect of these laws is that they were enacted by the British government on demand of the minorities in India before partition. The analysis and evaluation of these laws on Human Rights standards reveal that with the socio-economic development, these laws have become the main source for violations of the rights of minorities and specifically for the rights of their women i.e the "minority within minority." The strict laws for marriage and divorce are also cause for the conversion of minorities to Islam which a has very liberal and flexible

---

11. "A report on" 2006.
12. "A report on" 2007, 35–38.

approach to such laws. Feeling and admitting the gravity and sensitivity of the issue, the National Commission for Justice and Peace recommended their repeal by opining as follows:

> The main problem with these laws is their antiquity. These laws promulgated in pre-independence period, before the human rights standards were set, are redundant and source of human rights violations.[13]

Minority women are not only subjected to discrimination and disapproval by mainstream and Muslim laws but are also subjected to domestic violence as well as being subdued and humiliated by the customs, laws, and the patriarchal attitude of the followers of their own faith. They are victims of the violence of their own males. They are subjected to forced marriages. The result is conversion to Islam. They have to do dirty work as sweepers and low paid domestic workers in their locality. The domestic violence is wide spread. They are denied their right of succession to the property as well as free choice in marriage and separation.

However they are also socially condemned by Muslim society at large e.g. Muslims do not mix or socialize with them. Muslims do not dine or sit with them at the same table. They offer them food in separate dishes. Muslims do not allow them to work as cooks, but will hire them only for the dirty work of cleaning toilets or sweeping floors.

RECOMMENDATIONS

In view of this situation I recommend the following:

1. Inter-faith dialogues and inter-faith activities should be initiated at grass root level.

2. Socio-economic support:
   a. Social activities to be organized with main stream society.
   b. Women should be empowered through education, better employment and representation in government and local bodies. A quota should be reserved for women within minority quotas in all the electoral bodies and in employment.

3. Women should be encouraged to seek higher education so that they can get better jobs and come out of low paid jobs.

---

13. "A report on" 2007, 55.

4. Minorities may be exempted from the application of Islamic laws which create discrimination.

5. The minority laws which are the source of human rights violations should be reviewed to bring them in line with human rights standards.

9

Islamization of Laws in Pakistan and its Effect on Minorities

M. Aslam Khaki

In the name of God, the God of mankind, the God of all the Books and of all the Prophets. The God who bestowed His mercy upon His people by sending prophets to them so that they may take them to light from darkness, and from oppression to rehabilitation. The God who wished and willed to shower His bounties upon His creature by granting and protecting the rights of all the people and specially of the oppressed people on the basis of justice and fairness. The God who is at equal distance rather at no distance from all sections of His mankind. The God who does not see his mankind through the glasses of creed, color or race. The God who does not classify His people as majority and minority and hence has not provided any discriminatory laws for the non-Muslim minorities living in the Muslim states and also not for the Muslim minorities living in the non-Muslim states.

THE PROTECTION OF MINORITY rights is an old, worldwide problem and is not particular to any religion or region. Throughout history the majority has by and large always dominated and tended to subdue the minority. However in the twentieth century the problem has developed as an issue due to awareness and advocacy of human rights instruments and organizations. The minorities in various parts of the world are now demanding equal rights and Pakistan is no exception.

Non-Muslims in Muslim Majority Societies

According to the 1998 census 3.1% of Pakistan's population of 150 million belong to religious minorities.[1] Christians and Hindus are the main religious minorities.

Pakistan was created in the name of the religion Islam in 1947 by the division of united India. Thus since its birth the governments of Pakistan have tended to take steps towards Islamization of the country as well as of the society.

In 1977, one Chief of Army Staff, General Zia-ul-Haq, overthrew the popular democratic government of late Zulfiqar Ali Bhutto in the name of Islam. He felt himself duty-bound to take certain measures in the name of Islam to justify the change and also his position as unelected Chief Executive of the Government.

He gathered around him a large group of religious leaders to advise him how prevail upon the innocent, illiterate and emotional majority of Pakistan in the name of religion. These religious leaders advised him to enforce Islamic penal code in the country instead of first providing o cogent Islamic socio-economic environment which is, in fact, the prerequisite for an imposition of any Islamic punishments.

The enactments made and measures taken in the name of Islam were not *bonafide* but were *malafide* with ulterior motives.

It is pertinent to note that not only Zia-ul-Haq but all the governments in Pakistan, even the secular governments, used Islam as a shield for protecting their rule. Before the dawn of Zia-ul-Haq's fundamentalist regime the government of the most liberal and secular party in Pakistan under the leadership of Zulfiqar Ali Bhutto shamelessly surrendered before the Muslim clerics and declared Ahmadis (one of the sections claiming to be Muslims) as non-Muslims. Aggressive amendments were made in the Constitution as well as in the criminal laws to curse and curb them legally as well as socially. Since the creation of Pakistan this was the first victory of fundamentalist theocrats and it encouraged them to demand "more and more" in the name of Islam at the cost of minorities.

In 1977 General Zia-ul-Haq, after taking over the charge as Chief executive of civil as well as military organs, founded a factory of Ordinances and Acts on the wish and will of Muslim clerics. The Majlis-e-Shoora (Parliament) consisting of hand-picked and un-elected people rather unworthy of being elected, started stamping the Ordinances of Zia-

---

1. *Census of Pakistan.*

ul-Haq as laws and also gave great leeway for Zia-ul-Haq to corrupt the Constitution of Pakistan, the sacred document of the Pakistani nation. Consequently, many corruptions in the name of Islamization were made in the constitution as well as in the criminal law of the country.

By insertion of *Article 203–D*, a Federal Shariat Court was created to examine the laws within the framework of Islam and to declare them void if found repugnant to Islam. This supra-parliamentary power of Federal Shariat Court led to the production of discriminatory laws in Pakistan.

By making a series of amendments and inserting discriminatory laws in the law documents of Pakistan, the country *for* all the religious groups emerged as a land for Muslims or, rather, for 'Mullas' only.

THE CONSTITUTION

The Constitution of Pakistan from 1973[2] provides on one hand for the equality of all the citizens and for non-discrimination on the basis of sex, creed or race, etc. but on the other hand and, in the same breadth, it clearly and explicitly provides for discrimination against non-Muslims and for the supremacy of Muslims over non-Muslims.

To begin, here are a few articles from the sacred Constitution of Pakistan 1973 which provide for equality before the law and equal opportunities for all the citizens of Pakistan starting with *Article 4*:

> (1) To enjoy the protection of law and to be treated in accordance with law is the inalienable right of every citizen, wherever he may be, and of every other person for the time being within Pakistan. (...).

Article 25 regarding the equality of citizen states:

> (1) All citizens are equal before law and are entitled to equal protection of law.
>
> (2) There shall be no discrimination on the basis of sex alone.
>
> (3) Nothing in this Article shall prevent the State from making any special provision for the protection of women and children.

Article 27 aims at being a safeguard against discrimination in services, *Article 20* about freedom to profess religion, *Article 21* about safeguarding against taxation for purposes of any particular religion, *Article 22*

---

2. *Constitution of the Islamic.*

about safeguards as to educational institutions in respect of religion states respectively:

> (1) No citizen otherwise qualified for appointment in the service of Pakistan shall be discriminated against in respect of any such appointment on the ground only of race, religion, caste, sex, residence or place of birth.
>
> Subject to law, public order and morality:
>
> (a) every citizen shall have the right to profess, practice and propagate his religion; and
>
> (b) every religious denomination and every sect thereof shall have the right to establish, maintain and manage its religious institutions.
>
> No person shall be compelled to pay any special tax the proceeds of which are to be spent on the propagation or maintenance of any religion other than his own.
>
> (1) No person attending any educational institution shall be required to receive religious instruction, or take part in any religious ceremony, or attend religious worship, if such instruction, ceremony or worship relates to a religion other than his own.
>
> (2) In respect of any religious institution, there shall be no discrimination against any community in the granting of exemption or concession in relation to taxation.
>
> (3) Subject to law,
>
> (a) No religious community or denomination shall be prevented from providing religious instruction for pupils of that community or denomination in any educational institution maintained wholly by that community or denomination; and
>
> (b) No citizen shall be denied admission to any educational institution receiving aid from public revenues on the ground only of race, religion, caste or place of birth. (...)

Three more examples will be given through *Article 26* about non-discrimination in respect of access to public places, *Article 36* about the protection of minorities, and finally *Article 38* about the promotion of social and economic well-being of the people:

(1) In respect of access to places of public entertainment or resort, not intended for religious purposes only, there shall be no discrimination against any citizen on the ground only of race, religion, caste, sex, residence, or place of birth. (...)

The state shall safeguard the legitimate rights and interests of minorities, including their due representation in the Federal and Provincial services.

The State shall:

(a) Secure the well-being of the people, irrespective of sex, caste, creed or race, by raising their standard of living, by preventing the concentration of wealth and means of production and distribution in the hands of a few to the detriment of general interest and by ensuring equitable adjustment of rights between employers and employees, and landlords and tenants; (...)

(d) Provide basic necessities of life, such as food, clothing, housing, education and medical relief, for all such citizens, irrespective of sex, caste, creed or race, as are permanently or temporarily unable to earn their livelihood on account of infirmity, sickness, or unemployment; (...)

However, a plain study of the same Constitution of Pakistan reveals that the preceding fundamental rights as provided by the Constitution are just ornamental and not fundamental. All these rights are negated and stand as show *pieces* when confronted with the following articles in the same sacred document. These Constitutional provisions clearly provide for making the minorities second class citizens in term of rights and limit opportunities of participation in the government. *Article 31* deals with Islamic way of life:

(1) Steps shall be taken to enable the Muslims of Pakistan, individually and collectively, to order their lives in accordance with the fundamental principles and basic concepts of Islam and to provide facilities whereby they may be enabled to understand the meaning of life according to the Holy Quran and Sunnah.

(2) The state shall endeavour, as respects the Muslims of Pakistan:

(a) to make the teaching of the Holy Quran and Islamiat compulsory, to encourage and facilitate the learning of Arabic language and to secure correct and exact printing and publishing of the Holy Quran;

(b) to promote unity and the observance of the Islamic moral standards; and

(c) to secure the proper organization of zakat, [ushr,] auqaf and mosques.

Article 40 talks about strengthening bonds with the Muslim world and about promoting international peace:

> The State shall endeavour to preserve and strengthen fraternal relations among Muslim countries based on Islamic unity, support the common interests of the peoples of Asia. Africa and Latin America, promote international peace and security, foster goodwill and friendly relations among all nations, and encourage the settlement of international disputes by peaceful means.

The following article in the constitution, *Article 41*, is about the president:

> (1) There shall be a President of Pakistan who shall be the Head of State and shall represent the unity of the Republic.
>
> (2) A person shall not be qualified for election as president unless he is a Muslim of not less than forty-five years of age and is qualified to be elected as member of National Assembly. (...)

There is no article directly debarring a non-Muslim from becoming the Prime Minister, however, the oath of the Prime Minister requires him explicitly to be a committed Muslim. The relevant portion of his oath is found in *Article 42* in the third Schedule of the constitution:

> (In the Name of Allah, the most Beneficent, the most Merciful,)
>
> I, _____ , do swear solemnly that I am a Muslim and believe in the unity and Oneness of Almighty Allah, the Books of Allah, the Holy Quran being the last of them, the Prophethood of Muhammad (peace be upon him) as the last of the Prophets and that there can be no Prophet after him, the Day of Judgment, and all the requirements and teachings of the Holy Quran and Sunnah.

The third Schedule of the Constitution of Pakistan sets out the form of oaths of various constitutional offices from the office of President (*Article 42*) to the office of Prime Minister (*Article 91*), Federal Minister or Minister of State (*Article 92*), Speaker of National Assembly or Chairman of Senate (*Article 53.2* and *61*), Deputy Speaker of National Assembly or

Deputy Chairman of Senate (*Article 53* and *61*), members of the National Assembly or Member of Senate (*Article 65*), Governor of a province (*Article 102*), Chief Minister or Provincial Minister (*Article 131.4* and *132.2*), Speaker of a Provincial Assembly (*Article 53.2* and *127*), Deputy Speaker of a Provincial Assembly (*Article 53.2* and *127*), Member of a provincial Assembly (*Article 65* and *127*), Auditor General of Pakistan (*Article 168.2*), Chief Justice of Pakistan or a High Court or Judge of the Supreme Court or a High Court (*Article 178* and *194*), Chief Justice or Judge of the Federal Shairat Court (Article *203C.7*), Chief Election Commissioner (*Article 214*), and Members of the Armed Forces (*Article 244*). All these oaths have three Islamic components in common. These are the use of the following phrases:

1. "In the Name of Allah, the most beneficent, the most merciful" (Arabic text).

2. That I will strive to preserve the Islamic ideology which is the basis for the creation of Pakistan.

3. May Allah Almighty help and guide me (A'meen).

Article 203(2) of the Constitution provides that all the judges of the Federal Shariat Court shall be Muslims:

> The Court shall consist of not more than eight Muslim judges, including the Chief Justice, to be appointed by the president.

It is also pertinent to note that as per the legal rules, no non-Muslim lawyer can appear before the Federal Shariat Court or before the Shariat Appellate Bench of Supreme Court.

Part IX of the Constitution provides in *Article 228* for Islamic Provisions and creates an Islamic Ideological Council to advise the government on Islamization of laws. Furthermore, the Constitution in *Article 62* about qualification for members of Masjid-e-Shoorah (the Parliament) establishes:

> A person shall not be qualified to be elected or chosen as a member of Majlis-e-Shoora (Parliament) unless: (…)
>
> d) He is of good character and is not commonly known as one who violates Islamic Injunctions; (…)

Non-Muslims in Muslim Majority Societies

LAWS DEROGATORY TO MINORITY RIGHTS

The enactment and legislation of lawsin the name of Islamization in Pakistan has directly effected the rights of the minorities.

It is interesting to note that even though against Islamic doctrine the Hudood laws have been made almost equally applicable to both non-Muslims and Muslims, but as far as the right of "evidence" in these cases is concerned non-Muslims have not been considered trustworthy or reliable witnesses. *Section 8* of the Offence of Zina (Enforcement of Hudood) Ordinance 1979 provides for the proof of Hadd which requires:

> (b) at least four Muslim adult male witnesses, about whom the Court is satisfied, having regard to the requirements of tazkiyah al-shuhood, that they are truthful persons and abstain from major sins (*kabair*), give evidence as eye-witnesses of the act of penetration necessary to the offence:
>
> Provided that, if the accused is a non-Muslim, the eye-witnesses may be non-Muslims.[3]

Section 7 of the Offences Against Property (Enforcement of Hudood) Ordinance, 1979, while providing the proof for theft (liable to Hadd) comes up with the same conditions:

> (b) at least two Muslim adult male witnesses, other than the victim of the theft, about whom the Court is satisfied, having regard to the requirements of "tazkiyah-al-shuhood," that they are truthful persons and abstain from major sins (kabair), give evidence as eye-witnesses of the occurrence:
>
> Provided that, if the accused is a non-Muslim, the eye-witnesses may be non-Muslim: (...)[4]

Section 9 of the Prohibition (Enforcement of Hadd) Order, 1979, requires at least two Muslim adult male witnesses to prove the case as Hadd:

> (b) at least two Muslim adult male witnesses, about whom the Court is satisfied, having regard to the requirement of "tazkiyah ul-shuhood," that they are truthful persons and abstain from major sins (kabair) give evidence of the accused having committed the offence of drinking liable to hadd.[5]

---

3. *Offence of Zina*.
4. *Offences Against Property*.
5. *Prohibition*.

Islamization of Laws in Pakistan and its Effect on Minorities

In this article, "tazkiyah al-shuhood" means the mode of inquiry adopted by a Court to satisfy itself as to the credibility of a witness.

Section 6 of the Offence of Qazf (Enforcement of Hadd) Ordinance, 1979, provides that there must be two Muslim adult male witnesses to prove the case as Hadd. It states:

> (c) at least two Muslim adult male witnesses, other than the victim of the qazf, about whom the Court is satisfied, having regard to the requirements of tazkiyah al-shuhood that they are truthful persons and abstain from major sins (Kabair), give direct evidence of the commission of qazf:
>
> Provided that, if the accused in a non-Muslim, the witnesses may be non-Muslims.[6]

The law of Evidence of Pakistan Qanun-e-Shahadat Order, 1984, seriously discriminates against minorities (non-Muslims) as well as the women who appear as witnesses in most of the civil cases besides their dismissal in Qisas-o-Diyat and Hudood laws. *Articles 3* and *17* of the said Order are reproduced as follows:

> (...) Provided further that the Court shall determine the competence of a witness in accordance with the qualifications prescribed by the injunctions of Islam as laid down in the Holy Quran and Sunnah for a witness, and, where such witness is not forthcoming, the Court may take the evidence of a witness who may be available.
>
> (...)
>
> (1) The competence of a person to testify, and the number of witnesses required in any case shall be determined in accordance with the Injunctions of Islam as laid down in the Holy Qur,an and Sunnah.[7]

PAKISTAN PENAL CODE

Chapter XVI of the Pakistan Penal Code 1860 relating to Offences Affecting The Human Body was totally redesigned and substituted with the so called Islamic law of Qisas-o-Diyat. Article 299-238 (H) were introduced to substitute the existing sections on the subject. Though the

6. *Offence of Qazf.*
7. *Qanun-e-Shahadat.*

law provided for compromise in cases of murder and injuries which is inline with the modern trend of eliminating the death sentence, the law also opened the way to honour killing. The law was also made applicable to non-Muslims. For proof of murder (Qatl-I-amd) liable to Qisas, *Article 304* discriminates against non-Muslims appearing as witnesses.

> (1) Proof of qatl-i-amd shall be in any of the following forms, namely:
>
> (a) the accused makes before a Court competent to try the offence a voluntary and true confession of the commission of the offence; or
>
> (b) by the evidence as provided in Article 17 of the Qanun-e-Shalladat, 1984 (P.O. No. 10 of 1984).[8]

It is to be noted that *Article 17* of the Qanun-e-Shahadat, 1984, as referred to above provides for Islamic law of evidence by which the testimony of a non-Muslims is not accepted in Qisas.

Though religion is used as a tool and target in relation to minority rights the study of history reveals that it is not religion but the religious clerics who create the problems through their ulterior motives. Mishra and Kumar Singh opine the same:

> However, irrespective of these moral protections of various UN agencies, the atrocities on minorities has been true. It is not related with religion. It is directly related to maintain the status quo of the huge money of dominant classes of the society.[9]

Despite protections of national as well as international sacred documents, the minorities in Pakistan have been vehemently denied their rights in letter and spirit. The minorities have been treated as second class citizens by the law of the country, conduct of the people, and customs of the society. Ahmadis are at the fore of such legal discrimination, social humiliation, and court convictions. They are declared non-Muslims by the state and are banned to call or identify themselves as Muslims. Special penalty laws under *Article 298–A, B, and C* were introduced in the Pakistan Penal Code.

These laws speak a clear bias, or rather prejudice and are evidence of the heat of aggression and hatred against Ahmadis. *Article 298–B* in the

---

8. Pakistan Penal Code.
9. Mishra and Kumar Singh, *Status of Minorities*, 152.

Penal Code talks about misuse of epithets, descriptions and titles, etc., reserved for certain holy personages or places:

> (1) Any person of the Qadiani group or the Lahori group (who call themselves "Ahmadis") or by any other name who by words, either spoken or written, or by visible representation—
>
> a) refers to or addresses, any person, other than a Caliph or companion of the Holy Prophet Muhammad (Peace Be Upon Him), as "Ameer-ul-Mumineen," "Khalifat-ul-Mumineen," "Khalifat-ul-Muslimeen," "Sahaabi," or "Razi Allah Anho,"
>
> b) refers to, or addresses, any person, other than a wife of the Holy prophet Muhammad (Peace Be Upon Him), as Ummul-Mumineen;
>
> c) refers to, or addresses, any person, other than a member of the family "Ahle-bait" of the Holy Prophet Muhammad (Peace Be Upon Him), as "Ahle-Bait"; or
>
> d) refers to, or names, or calls, his place of worship a "Masjid";
>
> shall be punished with imprisonment of either description for a term which may extend to three years, and shall also be liable to fine.
>
> (2) Any person of the Qadiani group or Lahori group (who call themselves "Ahmadis" or by any other name) who by words, either spoken or written, or by visible representation, refers to the mode or form of call to prayers followed by his faith as "Azan" or recites Azan as used by the Muslims, shall be punished with imprisonment of either description for a term which may extend to three years and shall also be liable to fine.[10]

Concerning a person of the Qadiani or the Lahori group calling himself a Muslim or preaching or propagating his faith is treated under *Article 298-C* in the Penal Code:

> Any person of the Qadiani group or the Lahori group (who call themselves "Ahmadis" or by any other name,) who, directly or indirectly, poses himself as a Muslims, or calls, or refers to, his faith as Islam, or preaches or propagates his faith, or invites other to accept his faith, by words, either spoken or written, or by visible representations or in any manner whatsoever outrages the religious feelings of Muslims shall be punished with imprisonment of

---

10. *Pakistan Penal Code.*

either description for a term which may extend to three years and shall also be liable to fine.

Minorities as well as the liberal Muslims (a minority among the majority) have also been subjected to trials and convictions under Blasphemy Laws. A number of cases were registered against them. A concise list is shown by the tables.[11]

TABLE 1: Persons Formally Charged Under Blasphemy Laws 1986–2006

Religion	Registered cases	Charged and alleged
Muslim	197	414
Christian	76	96
Ahmadi	89	302
Hindu	7	12
Unknown	7	10
Total	376	834

TABLE 2: Persons Formally Charged Under Blasphemy Laws 2006

Religion	Registered cases	Charged and alleged
Muslim	27	38
Christian	6	7
Ahmadi	10	39
Hindu	-	-
Unknown	3	4
Total	46	88

The rights of minorities have been attacked in various aspects and form a variety of angles. The important right of freedom to profess and practice religion is protected by *Article 20* of the Constitution of the Islamic Republic of Pakistan as referred to above and also by the Universal Declaration of Human Rights, 1948, as envisaged in its *Article 18*:

> Everyone has the right to freedom of thought, conscience and religion; this right includes freedom to change his religion or belief, and freedom, either alone or in community with others and

---

11. "A report on" 2007, 38.

in pubic or private, to manifest his religion or belief in teaching, practice, worship and observance.[12]

In line and in elaboration of the said article, the Declaration on the Elimination of all Forms of Intolerance and Discrimination based on Religion and Belief sets out nine indicators as evidence of the fundamental right to freedom of religion and belief. *Article 6* claims:

> In accordance with Article 1 of the present Declaration, and subject to the provisions of Article 1, paragraph 3, the right to freedom of thought, conscience, religion or belief shall include, inter alia, the following freedoms:
>
> a. To worship or assemble in connection with a religion or belief, and to establish and maintain places for these purposes;
>
> b. To establish and maintain appropriate charitable or humanitarian institutions;
>
> c. To make, acquire and use to an adequate extent the necessary articles and materials related to the rites and customs of a religion or belief;
>
> d. To write, issue and disseminate relevant publications in these areas;
>
> e. To teach a religion or belief in places suitable for these purposes;
>
> f. To solicit and receive voluntary financial and other contributions from individuals and institutions;
>
> g. To train, appoint, elect or designate by succession appropriate leaders called for by the requirements and standards of any religion or belief;
>
> h. To observe days of rest and to celebrate holidays and ceremonies in accordance with the precepts of one's religion of belief;
>
> i. To establish and maintain communications with individuals and communities in matters of religion or belief at the national and international levels.[13]

---

12. *Universal Declaration.*
13. *Declaration on the Elimination.*

Besides Islamization in terms of legislation, the atmosphere of Pakistan is also corrupted by the orthodox customs and concepts, such as the concept tabled by Muslim clerics of the death penalty for apostasy (i.e conversion from Islam to any other religion).

Though there is no punishment for such a "religious offence" in Pakistani law, yet this belief has the force of law in the mind of general public of Pakistan. The religious clerics have been demanding the government to make it a law. The said belief, even without the support of law, has taken away the fundamental rights of the Muslim citizen to profess any religion (*Article 20*) as well as the right of minorities to be treated as equal citizens of Pakistan (*Article 25*).

At the social level, the belief about apostasy propagated by clerics is one of the main impediments in the way of real inter-faith harmony at the grassroots level and also in weaving a community of followers of different faiths.

The M.M.A (a syndicate of religious political parties), comprised of religious clerics, is in the governments of two of Pakistan's four provinces. In these provinces the Shari'ah Bill and the Hisba Bill and other legislation and rules of conduct for men, and especially for women have pushed the society into a Taliban-style regime.

Even without power of the government, some Muslim clerics heading the religious institutions have assumed control of the state within state. These people are initially encouraged by some government ministers and agencies for their ulterior political motives. Despite these institutions being a threat to minorities they are neither cursed nor curbed so long as they serve the purposes of the government. However, when they exceed their limits and become a threat to the political designs of the governments, then the government takes a serious notice of the situation. Reference is made to the recent events of Lal Masjid and Jamia Hafsa in the capital city of Pakistan.

On the cold behavior of government functionaries to the protection of minorities the Human Rights Commission of Pakistan (HRCP) opined:

> The State promoted violence by failing to act against those attacking non-Muslims or their properties.[14]

---

14. *State of Human Rights.*

Islamization of Laws in Pakistan and its Effect on Minorities

The above mentioned discriminatory laws and measures taken in the name of Islamization of the country did not only affect the legal rights of the minorities but have also infringed on their social rights as side-effects and as after-effects. The award of twenty marks for Hafz-i-Qur'an (learning the Qur'an by heart) towards the admission criteria for the professional educational institution in Pakistan provides evidence of the discriminatory attitude of the state towards non-Muslims.

The discriminatory legal atmosphere and especially the discriminatory content of textbooks have led people to think and classify every issue of their lives as Muslims vis-à-vis minority.

The atmosphere of visible and invisible feelings of hatred against minorities has marginalized and segregated them from the mainstream of Pakistani society. Christians are treated and labeled locally as *Chohray* or untouchables.

In Pakistan, one may not see Muslim and minority elders sitting in the same club, sharing one community hall, or dining at the same table using the same utensils. One can also hardly see the children of different faiths playing in the same park or sitting in the same desk in public schools. The dream of weaving together an inter-faith community cannot be realized in its true spirit without weeding out the discriminatory laws and differential attitudes in Pakistan.

RECOMMENDATIONS

Before parting with the topic, a few recommendations are put on the table for consideration:

1. The Inter-faith movements should direct their efforts towards taking legal steps against the discriminatory laws. i.e. by challenging these laws,

    a. On the floor of Parliament

    b. Before the Supreme Court of Pakistan under the Human Rights Chapter.

    c. Before Federal Shariat Court of Pakistan under *Article 203–D* of the Constitution of Pakistan.

2. Contents pertaining to a specific religion should be taken out of the textbooks of the educational institutions.

3. The specially purposed Institution of Islamization of law like the Islamic Ideology Council and the Federal Shariat Court ought to be abolished or, alternately, as a first step minorities be given representation in these bodies so that these institutions may not adopt any legislation which is against the rights of the minorities.

4. At the social level multi-faith hostels, clubs, and tours should be arranged for students to bring them in closer contact with each other.

5. A Multi-faith Council should be established in Pakistan to bring the people of different faiths into social harmony and also to investigate charges of blasphemy, defend the innocent accused and prevent inter-faith conflicts and clashes in society.

10

Non-Muslims in an Islamic State
A Case Study of Pakistan

Ahmad Salim

Although an Islamic state may be set up anywhere on earth, Islam does not seek to restrict human rights to the boundaries of such a state. Islam has laid down universal fundamental rights that are to be observed and respected in all circumstances. For example, human blood is sacred and may not be spilled without strong justification. It is not permissible to oppress women, children, minorities, old people, the sick or the wounded. Women's honor and chastity must be respected, the hungry must be fed, the naked clothed and the wounded or diseased treated medically irrespective of whether they belong to Islamic community or not. These provisions have been laid down in the Islamic State of Pakistan as fundamental rights for every citizen by virtue of her/his status as a human being.

Islam has also granted certain rights for non-Muslims who may be living in an Islamic state, and these rights must form part of the Islamic constitution. The life, property and honor of non-Muslim citizens are to be respected and protected in the same way as that of a Muslim citizen. There is no difference between a Muslim and a non-Muslim in civil or criminal law. And, every non-Muslim is to be regarded as eligible for a position of the highest responsibility without distinction of race, color, or class.

According to these principles, it becomes the primary responsibility of the Pakistani state not to interfere with the personal rights of non-

Muslims but to respect their freedom of conscience, belief, and the right to perform religious rites and ceremonies in their own way. Not only may they propagate their religion, they are also entitled to criticize Islam within the limits laid down by law and decency.

As well, even when a non-Muslim state oppresses its Muslim citizens, it is still not permissible for an Islamic state to retaliate against its non-Muslim citizens.

These rights are irrevocable and the non-Muslims cannot be deprived of them unless they renounce the covenant that grants them citizenship.

How does Islam view the concept of nation-state and the role of non-Muslims in an Islamic state? What are the grounds for or against constitutional and governances issues regarding non-Muslims in Pakistan? Perhaps this chapter will not answer these questions but will prepare us to discuss the discriminatory policies against non-Muslims in Pakistan with reference to governance, political participation, equitable constitutional issues, non-implementation of policies, social hatred, and biases.

NON-MUSLIMS IN AN ISLAMIC STATE: THE HISTORICAL MILIEU

The Muslim Perspective

In an Islamic state, non-Muslims are viewed as belonging to these two categories:

1. *Mu'ahidin* are those who have come under an Islamic state on account of a treaty, and have resolved to become a willing part of it without any political, ideological or social pressure.

2. *Dhimmiyyin* are those who have come under an Islamic state on account of being subdued in a battle, and so have had no other option

During the reign of Prophet Muhammad (PBUH), he signed a treaty with non-Muslims (Jews) that is commonly known as the "*Mithaq* of *Madinah*," at the time when Muslims migrated to *Madinah* and established a government there. Such pacts were signed with other nations as well.

If we study the "*Mithaq* of *Madinah*," it will become clear that the Jews who as *Mu'ahidin* accepted the Prophet (PBUH) as their ruler and were given the same rights as Muslims on the soil of Arabia. The treaty envisaged that the non-Muslims will be considered as one na-

Non-Muslims in an Islamic State

tion with Muslims in a political sense. As regards their religion, they will stand by theirs.

Dhimmiyyin, on the other hand, are those non-Muslim citizens of an Islamic state who have accepted its supremacy after being subjugated in a war. According to the *Qur'an*, if they give up their rebellious attitude and accept the sovereignty of the Islamic state by paying *Jiziyyah* (just as Muslim citizens had to pay *Zakat*) then they can become citizens and have their rights protected by the state.

> There is no differentiation between *Mu'ahidin* and *Dhimmiyyin* regarding their citizenship but both these groups have different rights. The rights of the *Mu'ahidin* cannot be decided solely by the Islamic government. Instead the final decision lies in the pact concluded between the two parties. On the other hand, the rights of the *Dhimmiyyin* have been decided by the Islamic law. These rights are a permanent part of the Islamic law. Just as the other decrees of the law are important in an Islamic state, in the same way protection and fulfillment of these rights is also essential and violation of these would be equivalent to deviation from religion.[1]

Therefore, non-Muslims have the right to their life, wealth and honor and the state is liable to protect these rights. In this context, the role of Pakistan as an Islamic state must be to practice the true teachings of Islam by ensuring its responsibility as the sole protector of its non-Muslim communities whether Christian, Buddhist, Hindu, Parsi or any other.

In an Islamic political order, every person enjoys the rights and powers of the Caliphate of God, and in this respect, all individuals are equal. No one can deprive anyone of her/his rights and powers. The agency for running the affairs of the state is to be established in accordance with the will of the individuals while the authority of the state will only be an extension of the powers of the individuals. Their opinion will be decisive in the formation of the government that will be run with their advice, and in accordance with their wishes. In this respect, the political system in Islam is a perfect democracy.

Legal Validation and the Minorities

According to state law and the international law of governance, all governments whether civilian or military, are responsible for building a soci-

---

1. Arnold, *The Preaching of Islam*, 80.

ety that strives to develop religious harmony and peace by protecting the rights of the minorities.

Pakistan being an Islamic state is bound to provide a system of governance where the rule of law ensures the protection and development of the Minorities as envisaged by its constitution in *Article 20*:

> a) Every citizen shall have the right to profess, practice and propagate his religion; and
>
> b) Every religious dominion and every sect therefore shall have the right to establish, maintain and manage its religious institution.[2]

Again, in a declaration on the elimination of all forms of intolerance and discrimination on religious beliefs, the Constitution of Pakistan discourages biases when it in *Article 33 and 36* says:

> The state shall safeguard the legitimate rights and interests of minorities, including their due representation in the Federal and Provincial services.
>
> *Protection of Minorities:* The state shall safeguard the legitimate rights and interests of minorities, including their due representation in the federal and provincial services.[3]

The constitutional framework and its provisions regarding the status of non-Muslims in Pakistan has been mentioned merely to show that neither state policy nor Islamic teachings deny the basic rights of minorities in Pakistan. Yet, these basic principles are continually being sidelined, rather pushed aside, to ensure that the minority question remains out of the mainstream of national life in the country. Regimes changed and decades have passed but these goals remain an illusive dream because the rulers failed to live up to their claims of equality.[4]

The present day Islamic states inevitably treat non-Muslim citizens as less than equal by curbing their access to power and religious freedom. Religious minorities in Pakistan suffer institutionalized discrimination because of the legalist orientation of the state and its obsession with Islamic jurisprudence. Some legalist positions in Islamic states are so strict that non-Muslims find it hard to live normal lives. Blasphemy laws and apostasy laws exemplify the hardships suffered by the minorities as

2. *Constitution of the Islamic.*
3. *Constitution of the Islamic.*
4. "A Report on" 2004, 7.

Non-Muslims in an Islamic State

well illustrating how seemingly democratic ideals of a religious state can easily be used to marginalize religious minorities.

GOVERNANCE AND CONSTITUTIONAL DISCRIMINATIONS

Before going into the details of constitutional and governance issues regarding discrimination and non-implementation of policies, it is vital to discuss the contemporary concepts of social security and its evolution. The term "social security" refers to the programs established by law to provide for the economic security and social welfare of its citizens and families.[5] According to this definition, it is the responsibility of the state to ensure the socio-economic security of the people without discriminating between the majority and minority communities.

Early Constitutional Discriminations

The first piece of legislation introduced in Pakistan was the *Objectives Resolution* that was passed by the Constituent Assembly in March 1949. This Resolution was a guideline to the Constituent Assembly to frame the Constitution of Pakistan. It was never meant to be a part of the Constitution nor was it the Ground Norm, or a cornerstone, of the political policy of the government.[6]

Yet in 1973, based on a recommendation of the Objectives Resolution, a major change was made in the Constitution. For the first time, "Islam shall be the State religion of Pakistan" was added to the Constitution.[7] Also, certain distinctions were made where Muslims were taken to be the majority while the non-Muslim citizens were taken as a minority.

When the concept of majority and minority is embedded and enshrined in such basic documents then the citizens who do not belong to the religion of the state will have to live discriminatory lives and experience perpetual fear. The 1973 Constitution thus created a permanent imbalance among the citizens of Pakistan.[8]

Though the first assault on the minorities and the beliefs of Quaid-e-Azam was made as early as 1949 when at the instance of Chaudhry Mohammad Ali, Liaquat Ali Khan got the Objectives Resolution passed

---

5. Calvert, *Social Security Law*, 5.
6. Shahani, "Discrimination in Laws."
7. *Constitution of the Islamic*.
8. Shahani, "Discrimination in Laws," 39.

by the Constituent Assembly.⁹ On March 7, the Prime Minster introduced the Bill, and faced strong opposition from the so-called minority members who, incidentally, were all Hindus. They were of the view that designating Pakistan as an Islamic state would place the minorities into the status of second class citizens.¹⁰

Following this, on February 27, 1953, anti Ahmaddiya riots began in Lahore. These riots were sparked by the Ahrars (A Muslim separatist movement) and were fully supported by Maulana Maudoodi and his Jamaat-i-Islami. The agitators issued a set of public demands that would declare the Ahmadis to be a non-Muslim community and that would cause the immediate removal of Zafrullah Khan from his post as the Foreign Minister. At the time, the agitators were calling upon central and provincial governments to dismiss all high-ranking Ahmadis from civil and military apparatus. Nazimuddin duly obtained the resignation of the Chief Minister, Dualtana.

Later, with the adoption of stern measures and by banning a number of religious-cum-political formations including the Ahrars, calm was finally restored to the province.¹¹

This discrimination was taken from the street to the constitution in 1973 with the inclusion of *Article 2*. During the Bhutto Government, with subsequent amendments to 1973 Constitution, a declaration against the Ahmadis as non-Muslims was passed. Bhutto also nationalized private institutions including institutions run by Christian missionaries and allocated separate seats for non-Muslim citizens in the Constitution for which the Electoral College was the members of National or Provincial Assemblies.

Earlier, a Committee on Fundamental Rights and on the Rights of the Minorities was formed by the Constituent Assembly in August 1947. In October 1953, when the Draft Constitution was being debated in the Constituent Assembly, the system of electorates was discussed and the Report of the Committee on the Fundamental Rights also came up before the Assembly. The one point on which differences arose within the committee, and on which some non-Muslim members added notes of dissent, was the issue relating to the system of separate electorates whose

---

9. Mughal, *Aqliyaten*, 14.
10. Nadeem, *Yeh Des Hamara*, 63.
11. Salim et al., "Violence, Memories," 172.

adoption had been recommended by the committee. B. C. Mandal, P. H. Burman and R. K. Chakravarty tendered a joint dissenting note stating that separate electorates were neither in the interest of the minorities nor would they be conducive to promoting the interests of the state.[12]

Zia-ul-Haq took over the government from Bhutto under a military dictatorship characterized by arbitrary policies. The first step he took that had a deep impact on non-Muslim communities, was the introduction of *Hudood Ordinances*. He created the Federal Shariat Court as a conferred appellate power for offences coming under Hudood laws.

By the end of 1970s, laws were constantly being framed to bring about an Islamic legal system. The Council of Islamic Ideology (CII) was reconstituted and made more powerful. On its recommendation, a set of four laws that came to be known as the Hudood Laws, were placed on the statute book. These were about prohibition of alcoholic drinks and other intoxicating drugs, theft and its punishments, rape and unlawful sexual intercourse, and Qazaf that deals with instances of false evidence about sexual relationships.[13]

Following the promulgation of Hudood Laws, a special Shariat Bench was constituted in every High Court, and an Appellate Bench was established in the Supreme Court. These benches were empowered to listen to appeals against convictions under Hudood by the Sessions' Judges, authorized to hear cases and appeals challenging a law as being in conflict with the Shariat, and were able to decide the matter with the proviso that the government could file an appeal with the Supreme Court if the conviction was struck down. It was made compulsory for the government to respect and honor the decisions taken by Shariat Courts.[14]

A Chronology of Constitutional Discrimination: 1949–2002[15]

1949—Objective Resolution was passed by the Constituent Assembly by opting to delegate to the state the responsibility to promote Islamic way of life, undermining Pakistan's identity as a multi-religious society. Despite the fact that non-Muslim communities had participated in the freedom struggle equally, the conservative and narrow mindset was encouraged to

---

12. Report of the Committee. 6.
13. Chaudhry, "Pakistan, Martial Law," 95–155.
14. Chaudhry, "Pakistan, Martial Law," 91.
15. "A Report on" 2002–2003.

raise questions as to whether non-Muslims were full citizens or liable to a special tax.

1953—Anti-Ahmadi riots were organized by the government in several cities of the Punjab. Martial Law was imposed in a few districts and the role of military bureaucracy was enhanced in politics.

1956—Although the move for a separate electorate was defeated, many Islamic provisions were included in the Constitution including the formation of an Advisory Council of Islamic Ideology to advise on bringing the laws in conformity with Islam.

1972—Nationalization of church educational institutions (including others).

1974—Ahmadis declared non-Muslims. Riots took place against Ahmadis.

1975—Reserved Seats introduced at national and provincial Assemblies by indirect elections (stress on religious identity).

1976—Islamic Studies was declared as compulsory subject. Liquor was banned for Muslims. Friday was made the weekly holiday.

1979—Introduction of Hudood and Zina Ordinances. Punjab government banned the recruitment of Christian nurses above their representation in the population. Separate Electorate introduced for Local Bodies elections. Zakat and Ushar (Islamic Taxes) ordinance passed that resulted in formulation of Tehreek-e-Nifaz-e-Jafferia (Shi'iat organization).

1980—Section 298-A added in the Penal Code (Blasphemy law).

1982—Section 295-B added in the Penal Code. Majlis-e-Shoora (consultative council) formed, minority representation shown in Majlis-e-Shoora.

1984—Islamic Law of Evidence introduced, reducing the value of court testimony of Muslim women and non-Muslim citizens to half of that of a Muslim male.

1985—A separate Electorate enforced through the 8th Amendment.

1986—Section 295-C was enacted by parliament. Churches and schools were attacked.

1988—Shariat Bill proposed in Senate.

1990—Federal Shariat court gives verdict on mandatory death penalty for Section 295-C. Qisas and Diyat Ordinance passed.

1991—Shariat Act was passed by the parliament. The personal law of non-Mulsims was not to be affected.

1992—The government tried to include a category for religion in the identity cards, some religious parties opposed it and some were in support.

1998—New Shariat Bill was passed in Parliament.

2000—Promise of abolition of separate electorate retained, provoking a massive protest in shape of boycott of Local Bodies elections.

2002—Joint electoral restored but religious identity in politics remained in the form of reserve seats in assemblies.

ISSUES OF GOVERNANCE AND POLITICAL PARTICIPATION

Equality of Citizens

Article 25 of the Constitution of Pakistan clearly lays down the equality of citizens as a guiding principle in the governance of the country:

1. All Citizens are equal before law and are entitled to equal protection of law
2. There shall be no discrimination on the basis of sex alone
3. Nothing in this article shall prevent the state from making any special provision for the protection of women and children.[16]

Regarding access to public office, the Universal Declaration of Human Rights of which Pakistan is a signatory, envisages in *Article 21* that:

1. Everyone has the right to take part in the government of his country, through freely chosen representatives
2. Everyone has the right of equal access to public service in his country
3. The will of the people shall be the basis of the authority of government; this will shall be expressed in periodic and genuine elections which shall be universal and equal suffrage and shall be held by secret vote or by equivalent free voting procedures.[17]

16. *Constitution of the Islamic.*
17. *Constitution of the Islamic.*

Non-Muslims in Muslim Majority Societies

Right to Participation

According to *Article 2* of the Declaration on the Rights of Persons Belonging to National or Ethnic, Religious and Linguistic Minorities, a person belonging to minorities have the right to participate effectively in decision making on national and regional levels concerning the minority to which they belong or the region in which they live, in a manner not incompatible with national legislation.

The history of struggle for minority rights in terms of participation in the political process whether in the shape of a voter or an elected representative, has a long history of political and constitutional prejudice.

Non-Muslims in Pakistan have suffered for decades under policies that institute discriminatory laws, breed intolerance, and cause sociopolitical subjugation thus usurping the basic rights of non-Muslims in shaping their political life in Pakistan as independent and equal citizens.

The introduction of a separate electorate system has enhanced religious intolerance and discrimination causing the minorities to demand the dissolution of this system. In this regard, tremendous efforts have been made during the past decades by minority groups to advocate their rights, by making appeals to the government, and mobilize public opinion.

In order to study the state responsibility and the rights of non-Muslims with reference to governance, it is important to consider the following provisions in the *Preamble* and in *Article 32* of the Constitution:

> (...) the state shall exercise its powers and authority through the chosen representatives of people (...) the principle of democracy, freedom, equality, tolerance and social justice, as enunciated by Islam, shall be fully observed

> (...) fundamental right [Shall be guaranteed] subject to law and public morality.

> The state shall encourage local government institutions composed of elected representatives of the areas concerned and within such institutions special representation will be given to peasants, workers and women.[18]

The issue of separate and joint electorates can be traced back in history to when the Government of India Act of 1935 was amended to provide for

---

18. *Constitution of the Islamic.*

separate electorates for Caste Hindus and Scheduled Castes within the Hindu community of East Bengal. After the Partition of Pakistan, no difficulty cropped up with regard to separate or joint electorates until 1952.

In August 1947 the Committee on Fundamental Rights and on the Rights of the Minorities was formed by the Constituent Assembly. In October 1953, when the Draft Constitution was being debated in the Constituent Assembly, the system of electorates also came under discussion. The one point on which differences arose within the Committee, and on which some non-Muslim members added notes of dissent, was about the system of separate electorates recommended by the Committee.[19]

Then in January 1956 the Ganatantri Dal withdrew its support of the coalition, followed by the Scheduled Castes Federation and the Pakistan National Congress. After that the Nizam-e-Islam Party directed its nominees on the cabinet to resign from it. That put an end to the ministry of the United Front, to be replaced on September 9, 1956 by a ministry of the Awami league. Along with this the League also succeeded in forming a coalition at the center in conjunction with the Republican Party. Fazlul Qadir Chaudhry (Muslim League) said in a statement:

> Joint electorates are sure to bring about the end of East Pakistan, that is East Pakistan and West Bengal will become one.[20]

When the voting took place in the Assembly on this issue, 159 votes were cast in favor of joint electorates and just one against it. Out of the 159 votes 59 came from Hindu members and 100 from the Muslims. This gave adherents of separate electorates the propaganda point that only 100 Muslim members had supported joint electorates out of a House of 237. Members of the depressed classes had always been in favor of joint electorates along with the concession of reserved seats, but at that stage the Speaker refused to allow any change in the resolution. Protesting against the ruling of the Speaker, members of the Scheduled Castes Federation walked out of the House.

> When the Electoral (Amendment) Bill, advocating joint electorates for the whole country, was moved in the National Assembly for discussion, two Christian members from West Pakistan, C. E. Gibbon and Joshua Fazluddin opposed it, while the Muslim League too appeared to be quite active. Gibbon insisted that the Christians should

---

19. Salim, *Religious Minorities*.
20. *East Pakistan Assembly*, 200.

be represented in the assemblies by men from the community itself. However, the prolonged battle that began in 1952 finally ended with victory of the joint electorates system in 1957.[21]

The new era of such political turmoil began in 1979 when the Local Bodies elections were ordered by General Zia-ul-Haq through Presidential Order Number 14 in 1985. This system was later approved by the parliament in the Eighth Constitutional Amendment.

As a result, the separate electorate system barred the citizens of Pakistan from voting for candidates not of their own religious identity in the General Elections of 1985, 1988, 1990, 1993, and 1997.

All four elections from 1988 to 1997 were held on the basis of separate electorates. This was actually a continuation of the mood set by General Zia though Benazir Bhutto did try to strike a different note in her second term by bidding to win over the minorities through the ruse of a double voting right.

Apart from that single attempt, the changing regimes of Pakistan People's Party and Pakistan Muslim League as well as the four interim set-ups, took no steps to do away with this injustice. Unfortunately, the minority representatives elected during 1988 to 1997 also failed to live up to the expectations of their people.[22]

> The religious minorities were only allowed to vote for a limited number of seats reserved for their communities: ten out of 217 in the National Assembly (lower house of the bicameral parliament) and twenty-three out of 483 members of the four Provincial Assemblies. While this electoral system undermined the polity and the social fabric in the country as a whole, the religious minorities suffered the worst social, political and economic damage for the past twenty-one years of this scheme of religio-political apartheid. This system of separate electorate violates the norms and principles of democratic governance and standards of universal adult franchise. Separate electorate break the promise made by Mohammad Ali Jinnah, the father of the Nation, in his inaugural speech to the Constituent Assembly of Pakistan on August 11, 1947: 'you may belong to any religion, caste or creed- that has nothing to do with the business of the state—now, I think we should keep that in front of us as our ideal and you will find that in course of time Hindus would cease to be Hindus and Muslims would cease to be Muslims,

21. Salim, *Religious Minorities*, 12–13.
22. Salim, *Religious Minorities*, 12–13.

Non-Muslims in an Islamic State

not in the religious sense, because that it the personal faith of each individual, but in the political sense as citizens of Pakistan.[23]

The struggles of the minorities for the restoration of a joint electorate begun in 1979, began to pay off during 2000–2001 when various organizations accelerated their efforts. Advocacy campaigns, written appeals and mobilization of public opinion in favor of a joint electorate system, and boycotting the local bodies system, made the government abolish separate electorates on January 16, 2002.

On August 1, 2002 the government restored reserved seats for religious minorities in National and Provincial Assemblies. These were the same number of seats as was reserved for all minorities in the separate electorate system for the National Assembly: four seats for Christians, four for Hindus, one for Sikh, Parsi and Buddhist communities, and one for Ahmadis.

A few years back National Assembly seats were increased from 217 to 350 to include 60 seats reserved for women and 25 for the technocrats.

The Hasba Bill passed in the NWFP, put in place a "Mohtasib" (ombudsman) to curb maladministration, to guard public morality and etiquette in the province, andto ensure that Islamic values were respected. This bill was also perceived by minority communities as a potential tool for further harassment. In August, the Supreme Court—after a Constitutional Reference filed by President Parvez Musharraf—ruled that some clauses of the controversial Hasba Bill were unconstitutional advising the NWFP Governor to not sign the Bill.

SOCIAL BIASES VIOLATE THE CONCEPT OF EQUALITY

Social biases and hatred are entrenched in Pakistani society in the shape of laws and regulations, and especially in the articles and provisions of the Constitution where discrimination against religious minorities is apparent. Of these, some items are meant to create a preferential space for Muslim citizens while the others just ignore the fact that Pakistan is a multi-religious society.

The following are examples of biases and discrimination maintained in the Constitution of Pakistan. *Article 2* states "Islam to be the state religion" and *Article 41 (2)* "The head of the State has to be a Muslim."

---

23. "A Report on" 2001, 74.

This constitutional and legislative approach is a statutory endorsement of discrimination in politics that provides strong bases for political instability because the very principle of equality is compromised in perhaps the most authentic national document of the country.[24]

Social Biases and Hatred: Constitutional and Social Abhorrence

Social biases against non-Muslims have manifested in different shapes during different regimes in Pakistan. Formal and informal discrimination against minorities has gone hand in hand as one has encouraged and deepened the other. Separate electorates disenfranchised and marginalized the minorities confirming their sense of being second-class citizens. Mainstream political parties have no interest in courting minorities or embracing prominent members and leaders of minority groups because they can not vote for them.

Paradoxically, it was during Bhutto's government when at the end of his rule he imposed religious order by closing nightclubs and racecourses, introducing prohibition and changing the weekly holiday from Sunday to Friday. When Zia took over, he introduced Hudood Ordinances relating to the offences of Zina (fornication), prohibition of liquor, offences of the theft of the property, and offences relating to Qazf (False accusation of adultery).

Social prejudice had become so strong that no party would support a non-Muslim candidate against a rival Muslim candidate. Placing non-Muslims in another category in electoral politics further deepened their sense of alienation.

Minorities were then left to form their own parties though only Christians took the opportunity. Other minorities have notable figures but no political organizations. Minority groups never supported separate electorates and have, for decades, struggled with whatever meager political capital they had to restore joint electorates in the hopes that that may help maintain a healthy balance in the mainstream political environment.

Inflaming Hatred through Media

The history of Pakistan is filled with disgraceful stories of social bias and hatred against minorities. The role played by political and religious par-

---

24. "A report on" 2002–2003, 93.

ties and dictatorial regimes in the victimization of the minorities is long. A few of them are listed here.

In the electronic media controlled by the government the representation of minorities has always been minimal. Even in the time of Junejo they could not get more than a routine item of half an hour on radio and television to celebrate their religious events. Even that half an hour was hampered by all kinds of restrictions such as that the image of Jesus Christ could not be shown on Pakistan Television (PTV).[25]

The National Commission for Justice and Peace (NCJP), in its Eighth Human Rights Monitor, released a report on "The Situation of Religious Minorities in Pakistan" where it is stated that the PTV serials "Mohammed Bin Qasim," "Shaheen," and "Tipu Sultan" were clear misrepresentation of historical events carried out to the disadvantage of non-Muslim minorities.

A national Urdu daily wrote in its October 20 editorial that a Christian Pastor, Peter Robertson, associated with a correspondence school was converting Pakistanis to Christianity and operating from Mianwali since 1995. He had converted 17,000 Muslims all over Pakistan. The paper said he used good looking young boys and girls for the purpose and urged clerics to 'wake up to the threat.'

> Within 22 days of the printing of this editorial, Churches and Christian property were burnt at Sangla Hill on the pretext of desecration of the holy Quran. Liberal Muslims remained silent and there was no protest or condemnation by Muslims at large. After the incident, Dr Sarfraz Naeemi, secretary of Tanzimat Madaris-e-Deeniya said the Christian clergy had set the churches on fire after the alleged desecration, "like they did in Shantinagar" (a Christian majority village that was burnt by Muslims because of an alleged desecration of the Holy Quran).[26]

According to a recent report by the NCJP, the commission monitored four major national Urdu dailies from August to October 2005 finding provocative news reports, statements and editorials against religious minorities including Christians, Hindus, Ahmadis and even Jews (hate in absentia).[27]

---

25. *Pakistan, Human Rights*, 100.
26. Waqar, "Hate mongering."
27. "A Report on ... 2006."

Non-Muslims in Muslim Majority Societies

Religiously Motivated Hate Speeches

Speakers in rallies organized by extremist and radical elements make provocative speeches against the minorities.

A common hate speech method is to use derogatory terms for minorities. Ahmadis are called "Qadiani" or "Mirzai" while Christians are called "Isai." These terms are not even considered derogatory by some.[28]

Employment Opportunities

In another NCJP report, the following is expounded.

> (. . .)Non-Muslim laborers, be they domestics, factory or farm workers, are an easy target of the malice of the profit hungry employers. The human rights violation and unequal treatment as workers at times, is even worse in the government services than private sector. The existing safeguards lack implementation and there is need of more appropriate legislation. However it is no coincident that sectors having bonded labor, low wages, and a lack of or no social security, also have a high concentration of minority laborers. It is so in the agriculture, brick-kiln factories, sanitation work, carpet weaving and domestic servitude. Similarly there is no denying the fact that non-Muslims enjoyed on paper the constitutional protection for employment in government service, but in actual fact, they were always subjected to discrimination.[29]

Workers of Christian-majority unions complained that not one of its members had been allotted any plot in Pakistan Railway's housing schemes.

In Bahawalpur, three Christian sweepers were obliged to go down into a gutter to clean it. They later died of gas poisoning while municipal authorities there knew of the presence of poisoned gas in the gutter.

Three Hindus were abducted in Dadu including a fifteen-year old boy called Dharampal. On the inability of their relatives to pay the ransom all three were killed.

In another case, ninety Hindu laborers were taken away by landlords and were released only after receiving ransom money.

In a village of Bheels near Ghotki, a number of Hindu women were abducted including a girl of twelve named Maruti who was subjected to

---

28. Waqar, "Hate mongering."
29. "A Report on . . . 2006."

forcible sex. No FIR was registered by the police because some government officials were also involved.

In another case, two Hindu sisters had been recovered from drug smugglers and instead of being protected as witnesses, were implicated in cases of unlawful sex.

Another grave problem relates to the location and construction of places of worship. There are cases where after giving permission to build the work was stopped half-way on government orders. An incident of this kind took place in Bahawalpur where work at an advanced stage on the construction of a church was stopped despite the fact that the government had itself granted permission to build at that location. In addition, there was no effort on the part of the authorities to compensate the resultant financial loss suffered by the Christian communities.[30]

The education policy has gone from bad to worse over the years. The syllabus is not based on democratic values, and the behavior of teachers is also discriminatory to non-Muslim students. In many government schools, in the absence of alternative arrangements, Christian children were obliged to study Islamiyat.

Despite the restoration of joint electorates, separate polling booths for Muslim and non-Muslim voters were retained in Lahore. The Ahmadis were still denied participation in the joint electorate, and in many cases, non-Muslim candidates were given symbols such as a dog, rat or a snake that are taken as degrading.

INTER-FAITH DIALOGUE IN THE ISLAMIC REPUBLIC OF PAKISTAN

Challenges and Prospects

Many Asian countries are beset with violent conflicts involving minorities where religion is a common cause of complex and ongoing disputes. Similarly, the challenges faced by non-Muslim communities in Pakistan are continuous and multifaceted.

The plight for minority rights has always remained crucial in determining the existing state structure. In this regard, incredible efforts were made, especially by religious minority organizations and coalition bodies

---

30. *Pakistan, Human Rights*, 100.

involving several CBOs and NGOs, to organize protests and demonstration in a concerted political effort to raise voices for human rights.

A brief overview of the situation of Christians in Pakistan reveals how the Christian community is subjected to severe physical, political, social, economic, and cultural oppression as it experiences the violation of its rights within its home country.

A denial of religious minority rights in Pakistan is often half-hidden and subtle, and may include limited access to education and employment opportunities leading to the perpetuation of poverty. In other instances, it takes the form of intimidation and violence by the state or by majority groups. This situation can be summarized as follows.

Firstly, the key challenge faced by minorities in Pakistan is that religion that is often used here as a tool of political oppression against the minorities as well as to assert the national identity of the majority groups. In this context, the pronounced actions of the extremists when coupled with the Islamization of policies have caused further deterioration. The manner in which secular values are being denied by the extremists has threatening implications for religious minorities, the civil society, and all the vulnerable groups within minorities such as women, disabled persons, under-privileged people, and children.

Secondly, just like other countries of South Asia, Pakistan also grapples with low literacy rates, especially in minority communities. Another issue is the problem of biased curriculum content that either distorts history by excluding the achievements of religious minority communities or breeds hatred through specific anti-minority rhetoric in the textbooks. There is also apprehension about unregulated religious schools called *madrassahs* in Pakistan. These schools promote extremist ideology to exploit the social fabric of the society. The young generation is taught the lessons of hatred by calling them infidels and projecting that some Christian schools impart fundamentalist views. This type of indoctrination is perceived to be a root cause of religious intolerance that has led to a rise in communalism across South Asia.

Thirdly, constitutional rights and legal validation are also a big challenge faced by minorities in Pakistan as the Constitution, substantive laws, and several regulations discriminate against citizens on the basis of religion. These provisions create a preferential status for Muslim citizens, ignoring the fact that Pakistan is a multi-religious society. These articles and laws need to be looked into in order to understand and resolve the present crisis.[31]

Prospects of Inter-Faith Dialogue in Pakistan

Petition campaigns were undertaken throughout the country to build consensus among people of all walks of life and all religions in villages, towns and cities. On various occasions, all-party conferences and awareness seminars were organized to form a basic agenda for justice. These efforts brought people of all faiths together to deliberate upon the issue faced by society.

The concept of inter-faith dialogue encompasses inter-faith harmony and peaceful coexistence among different communities, religions, sects and identities. People from different walks of life such as academicians, religious scholars, political leaders and workers, and members of governmental and non-governmental organizations took part in discussions.

Undoubtedly, the need for religious harmony and inter-faith dialogue is imperative for Pakistan, where sectarian killings and socio-political exploitation of minorities has widened the gulf by perpetuating hatred between the majority and minority groups.

In analyzing the present situation in the country, sincere efforts must be made to build an environment of greater tolerance and harmony at both individual and institutional levels.

1. All institutions must promote religious tolerance as an essential value. This religious tolerance must be based on positive aspects of different religions to ensure that the commonalities are shared.

2. Leaders of both religious and political parties must ensure religious harmony in their practices, speeches and actions because an approach of political bias, affiliation or self-centered interest will further worsen the situation. A dialogue on universal human issues needs to be carried out by our religious scholars and academicians.

3. Sectarian violence must be curbed by enforcing laws against keeping arms, stopping militant training, and confronting the growth of biased religious beliefs.

The dilemma associated with inter-faith dialogue is that the issues vital to inter-faith harmony, social justice, and peaceful coexistence may still be

31. "A Report on" 2007, 49.

overlooked. Muslims being the majority have power over decision-making and policy implementation but have not yet tried to eliminate discriminatory laws such as the Blasphemy law and other atrocious formations. The majority has neither developed an environment to discuss this issue with mutual consent nor has it invited the minority groups to suggest a policy that is acceptable to minority groups.

Other discriminatory laws affecting inter-faith relations continue to have a sanctioned status in the statutes. The Criminal Law Amendment Act 2006 (Women Protection Bill) sheepishly ignored the blatant religious discrimination in the Hudood laws where only Muslim judges can hear the Hudood cases even though the law is equally applicable to non-Muslims. The appeal court remains to be the Federal Shariat Court where a non-Muslim can not be a judge, lawyer or a witness.[32]

The need for inter-faith dialogue is immense in Pakistan. Consultation with different minority groups will definitely encourage understanding and co-operation between different religious communities. The effort to work toward a peaceful development with a mutual consent is an immediate need.

In Pakistan, the inter-faith dialogue must involve an attitude of love, tolerance and acceptance since inter-faith dialogue as a worldwide movement is the only available option to develop a cohesive understanding, mutual cooperation and peace in the society. The dialogue may commence on two levels:

1. Dialogue on social and communal harmony between majority and minority groups in order to create a sense of commitment for the global values of peace, harmony, cooperation and collective security by abandoning policies that are based on bias, ignorance or narrow self-interests thus decreasing gaps between various population groups.

2. Dialogue in minority groups at social, economic, cultural and political levels through an organized intellectual effort based clearly on the principles of equality, co-existence and compassion.

The coordinated efforts to develop an environment for inter-faith harmony can begin by pooling the ideas of people of every religion, and to

---

32. "A report on" 2007.

jointly analyze and develop appropriate strategies for the promotion of minority rights.

The nation-wide consultation and inter-faith discourse is also essential to provide a forum to help establish a nation-wide activist network and a lobbying body on minority rights. This, in turn, would definitely help in developing and shaping the future direction of inter-faith efforts for the benefit of religious minorities in Pakistan.

11

Possible Strategies for Religious Communities under Threat[1]

Kajsa Ahlstrand

AS AN EXAMPLE OF how religious communities may react to threats the following is presented as a sketch of possible strategies in the contemporary world. It gives a Christian understanding of strategies for religious communities under threat, but similar outlines can be presented by other religious traditions.

It is an incontrovertible fact that today there are Christians who are persecuted or threatened. Some are attacked because they openly profess their belief in Jesus Christ, others because their faith has led them to act in solidarity with oppressed groups and individuals. Thus, it has become impossible to distinguish between persecution for the sake of love of Christ and persecution for the sake of love of neighbor. This discussion begins to explore how Christians who find themselves under attack from neighbors of other faiths might react and act.

Many Christians, especially those living where Christianity has been closely linked to political power, find it difficult to accept that Christians in other parts of the world must struggle to survive both as individuals and as communities. They are convinced that it is possible to defend both the rights of non-Christians in Christian majority countries and the rights of Christians in countries where they are in minority. Freedom of religion is a universal human right, and Christians can only be credible in

1. This part has been sketched in a workshop set up by the Lutheran World Federation, January 2008. A slightly different version has been published in Bloomquist, *Identity, Survival*.

Possible Strategies for Religious Communities under Threat

defending this right if they, when in the majority, are as concerned with the rights of religious minorities as they also are committed to defend the right of Christians to practice their faith. Christians from established and mainline churches have generally been less open to the plights of minority Christians than Christians who come from dissenter churches.

We should neither ignore nor overestimate the threats that Christians in various parts of the world encounter from members of other religious communities. Fr Dan Madigan SJ has rightly commented in his response to *A Common Word*, the dialogue initiative by 138 Muslim leaders and scholars, that

> Over the centuries of undeniable conflict and contestation between members of our two traditions, each group has had its own internal conflicts that have claimed and continue to claim many more lives than inter-confessional strife. More Muslims are killed daily by other Muslims than by Christians or anyone else. The huge numbers who went to their deaths in the Iran-Iraq war of the 1980's were virtually all Muslims. Scarcely any of the tens of millions of Christians who have died in European wars over the centuries were killed by Muslims. The greatest shame of the last century was the killing of millions of Jews by Christians conditioned by their own long tradition of anti-Semitism and seduced by a virulently nationalist and racist new ideology. The last 15 years in Africa have seen millions of Christians slaughtered in horrendous civil wars by their fellow believers. A Catholic missionary is dozens of times more likely to be killed in largely Catholic Latin America than anywhere in the Muslim world.[2]

While this remark puts the conflicts between Christians and Muslims into perspective, it is still necessary to address situations where Christians are indeed under attack, by religious and/or political adversaries. "Religious adversaries" should not be taken to allude to Muslims only; other religious communities, e.g. politicized Hindu groups have also targeted Christians. On the one hand, Jesus taught his disciples to love their enemies, to turn the other cheek and to walk the extra mile. On the other hand, Christians who live as vulnerable communities among neighbors or systems that target them for persecution have the same right as any other group to defend

---

2. Madigan is an Australian Jesuit, founder of the Institute for the Study of Religions at the Pontifical Gregorian University, Rome, and member of the Vatican's Commission for Religious Relations with Muslims. The full text can be read at, Madigan, *A Common Word*.

themselves. How Christians have solved this dilemma varies according to particular situations and historical circumstances. We will here mention some of the tactics that Christians have employed. This is only the beginning of a theological-ethical agenda that needs to be pursued further.

MARTYRDOM

This strategy has been theologically tested and also practiced throughout the centuries. The classical image of the martyr is someone who is placed in a situation where they can either choose to hold on to their Christian faith and be killed or to renounce their faith and be spared. Faced with this choice, martyrs witness their allegiance to Christ with their blood. St Stephen in the Acts of the Apostles is the first martyr. Every martyr imitates Jesus in their readiness to embrace death rather than to betray their faith. There is no doubt that martyrdom is the exemplary Christian option in face of persecution, but martyrdom can never be a recommended strategy. It is very rare that the situation of persecution is as unambiguous as in the case of St Stephen. Although martyrdom may always be a possibility it is never to be sought out; to aspire to become a martyr is tantamount to spiritual hubris. Martyrdom might be encountered on the way of striving for justice and life for others, but martyrdom itself cannot be the strategy. In the common Christian heritage, martyrs are regarded as saints. Protestant traditions understand sainthood as someone who in their life and sometimes also in their death points to Jesus in such a way that others rejoice in the knowledge that God's grace is present in the world. But one cannot choose to be a saint; it is others who may come to recognize a life as being saintly.

AVOIDING CONFLICT

It has often been the case that Christians who are threatened or persecuted have chosen strategies that will reduce opportunities of contact with the persecutors. One way of doing this is physically to remove a Christian community from contacts with "outsiders" by creating a separate society of Christian villages, schools, hospitals etc. Another way is to make sure that Christians do not marry outside the Christian community, and that the faith is kept within the community rather than bearing witness to the faith in encounters with strangers. In some cases the faith has been kept as a private secret and denied when outsiders have inquired. For example, the

Possible Strategies for Religious Communities under Threat

Christian faith has been kept this way for generations by some Japanese Christians. Although this is how the faith has survived in some extreme circumstances, and judgment should not be passed on Christians who have chosen this strategy to retain their faith, the faith normally needs a wider community and to be openly proclaimed and practiced in order to contribute to human flourishing.

NON-VIOLENT RESISTANCE

In the Sermon on the Mount, Jesus urges his followers to "love your enemies." In spite of our failures to live up to this ideal, it remains the preferred strategy for Christians when they are under attack. The strategies of non-violence have developed methods to realize this. Non-violence is grounded in the gospel, but in situations where churches have been aligned with political power, resistance to power, even if non-violent, was not encouraged. It is a shameful fact that historically many churches in Europe have been so close to political power that they have failed to encourage theologies and practices that challenge the power. It belonged mainly to the dissenter churches such as the Society of Friends (the Quakers) to develop and practice non-violent Christian resistance to oppressive political power, which often operated under the name of the Christian regime or empire.

During the twentieth century, the two best known proponents of this strategy were M. K. Gandhi and Dr Martin Luther King, Jr. Non-violent resistance is not limited to people of the same faith, but seeks to include all who strive for a just society where the human rights for all citizens are respected.

One of the theological presuppositions of non-violent resistance is that since Christians are urged to love their enemies, they should help their attackers to realize that the violence they are inflicting is harmful not only to those who are attacked but also to the attacker. If the attacker can see the wrongfulness of their actions, the persecuted are spared and the attacker is converted to a better way of life. Thus, a foundation for a just and peaceful society is laid. Non-violent resistance can take many forms: peaceful demonstrations: hunger strikes, public debates, sanctions, legal actions, education, boycotts, lobbying etc. Recently, the tactic of international accompaniment has come to the fore. It has for example been used in Guatemala since the mid-1980s as international activists have accompanied returning Guatemalan refugees and monitored investigations into genocides perpetrated during the years of terror in the early 1980s as well as recent human rights violations. Currently there is an ecumenical program of accompaniment in Palestine, the purpose of which is to accompany Palestinians and Israelis in their non-violent actions and to carry out concerted advocacy efforts to end the occupation. Participants in the program monitor and report violations of human rights and international humanitarian law, support acts of non-violent resistance alongside local Christian and Muslim Palestinians and Israeli peace activists, offer protection through non-violent presence, engage in public policy advocacy and, in general, stand in solidarity with the churches and all those struggling against the occupation.[3]

LEGITIMATE SELF-DEFENSE

This strategy comes close to the "just war" thinking. Christians, like others, have the right to defend themselves when they are attacked. The classical just war doctrine addresses nations, not religious communities, but it can be adapted to a broader use. The doctrine can be presented this way:

> The damage inflicted by the aggressor on the nation or community of nations must be lasting, grave, and certain; all other means of putting an end to it must have been shown to be impractical or ineffective; there must be serious prospects of success; the use of arms must not produce evils and disorders graver than the evil to be eliminated. The power of modern means of destruction weighs very heavily in evaluating this condition.[4]

The most important point here is that violence is the last resort; all other means to reach a just solution must have been tried before a community may decide that armed self-defense is the lesser evil. Many would argue that we can never exhaust the possibilities of non-violent resistance and that non-violence thus remains the only permissible way for Christians under attack.

MEASURED ATTACK

Is it permissible for Christians to attack an aggressor? In the history of the church this has been addressed in terms of the legitimacy of tyrannicide.

3. At http://eappi.oikoumene.org/en/about/overview.html.

4. Paragraph 2309 of the Catechism of the Catholic Church, at http://www.catholic.com/library/Just_war_Doctrine_1.asp.

Possible Strategies for Religious Communities under Threat

This reasoning took place in medieval Europe, with regard to a Christian ruler whose power was thought to be God-given and thus responsible to God, but who turned into a tyrant. Medieval theologians identified two types of tyrants: usurpers and oppressors. The case of the usurpers was less complicated: because they did not rule legitimately, they should be deposed and punished (by capital punishment). In the case when the oppressors had come into power legitimately but later begun to oppress the people the medieval theologians were much less prone to allow the tyrant to be deposed and killed. The people should try to bear with the tyrant and put him right. Only if everything else failed and the cruelty of the tyrant was excessive did some theologians allow the tyrant to be killed. An example of a theologically motivated attempt at tyrannicide from the twentieth century is the group of Christians in Germany who conspired to kill Hitler.

Most Christians who today are under attack risk retaliation, not only for themselves but for the entire community, and a spiral of violence if they resort to violence in the form of tyrannicide. The criterion of a "serious prospects of success" is rarely the case if a minority group takes upon itself to attack oppressors from a majority group. This course of action is to be rejected both because it is dangerous as it may lead to more violence, and because it implies that individuals take upon themselves to both judge and execute capital punishment.

It is cynical to the extreme if Christians who live in societies where they can enjoy freedom of religion demand that Christians who are persecuted should vicariously witness with their lives to Christ. It is also quite irresponsible to encourage Christians in difficult situations to resort to violence. Christians, irrespective of where they live, need to study and train for non-violent responses to persecution and religiously motivated violence. This implies a readiness for those of us who live in safety to listen attentively to and also share the lives and the struggles of those who now strive to defend their rights to live as Christians in face of their adversaries.

Bibliography

"Agenda Item: 3 (a)." *National Commission for Justice and Peace-Pakistan.* UN Commission on Human Rights Working Group on Minorities. Tenth Session, March 1-5, 2004. Online: http://www.unhchr.ch/minorities/statements10/NCJP3a.doc.

The All-Pakistan legal decisions. Lahore: PLD Publishers, 1989.

"Amended Basic Law." *Palestine Official Gazette.* Special issue No. 2, (March 19, 2003).

Apostolov, Mario. *Religious Minorities, Nation States and Security. Five cases from the Balkans and the Eastern Mediterranean.* Aldershot: Ashgate, 2001.

"Arab Charter on Human Rights." *The League of Arab States,* 1997. Online: http://www1.umn.edu/humanrts/instree/arabhrcharter.html.

The Arab Human Development Report 2002. New York: United Nations Development Programme, 2002.

The Arab Human Development Report 2003. New York: United Nations Development Programme, 2003.

The Arab Human Development Report 2004. New York: United Nations Development Programme, 2004.

Arab Network for NGOs. Online: http://www.shabakaegypt.org/INDEX.asp.

"A Report on the Religious Minorities in Pakistan." *Human Rights Monitor 2001.* Lahore: National Commission for Justice & Peace Catholic Bishops' Conference of Pakistan, 2001.

"A Report on the Religious Minorities in Pakistan." *Human Rights Monitor 2002-2003.* Lahore: National Commission for Justice & Peace Catholic Bishops' Conference of Pakistan, 2003.

"A Report on the Religious Minorities in Pakistan." *Human Rights Monitor 2004.* Lahore: National Commission for Justice & Peace Catholic Bishops' Conference of Pakistan, 2004.

"A Report on the Religious Minorities in Pakistan." *Human Rights Monitor 2006.* Lahore: National Commission for Justice & Peace Catholic Bishops' Conference of Pakistan, 2006.

"A Report on Religious Minorities in Pakistan." *Human Rights Monitor 2007.* National Commission for Justice and Peace (Pakistan Catholic Bishops' Conference), 2007.

Arnold, Sir Thomas W. *The Preaching of Islam: A History of the Propagation of the Muslim Faith.*" London: Westminster A. Constable & Co., 1896.

"A short History of Church in Pakistan." *I.I.S.I.C Bulletin* (August/September 1995).

Ateek, Naim Stifan. *Justice, and Only Justice: a Palestinian Theology of Liberation.* Maryknoll: Orbis Books, 1989.

Barret, David B., et al. *World Christian Encyclopedia—A comparative survey of churches and religions in the modern world.* Volume 1: The world by countries, religionists,

Bibliography

churches and ministries. Volume 2: The world by segments: religions, peoples, languages, cities, topics. Oxford: Oxford University Press, 2001.

"Basic Agreement between the Holy See and the PLO," *Journal of Palestine Studies* issue 115 (Spring 2000). Also, *Jerusalem Quarterly* issue 8, (2000).

"Basic Law." *Palestine Official Gazette.* Special issue, (July 7, 2002). Online: http://muqtafi.birzeit.edu/mainleg/14138.htm.

Beehner, Lionel. "Shia Muslims in the Mideast." *Council on Foreign Relations 2008.* Online: http://www.cfr.org/publication/10903/shiite_muslims_in_the_middle_east.html.

Bengion, Ofra, and Gabriel Ben-Dor. *Minorities and the State in the Arab World.* London: Boulder, 1999.

Bijsterveld, Sophie van. "Equal Treatment of Religions? An international and comparative perspective." In, *Religious Pluralism and Human Rights in Europe: Where to Draw the Line?* edited by M. L. P. Loenen, and J. E. Goldschmidt. Antwerpen, Oxford: Inersentia, 2007.

"Blasphemy Law under Fire amid Religious Violence in Pakistan." *Christian Today* (May 4, 2007). Online: http://www.christiantoday.com/article/blasphemy.law.under.fire.amid.religious.violence.in%20pakistan/10620.htm.

Bloomquist, Karen L. *Identity, Survival, Witness: Reconfiguring Theological Agendas.* Geneva: The Lutheran World Federation, 2008.

Broude, Benjamin, and Bernard Lewis. *Christians and Jews in the Ottoman Empire: The Functioning of a Plural Society.* Volume 1, New York: Holmes & Meier, 1982.

Calvert, Harry. *Social Security Law.* London: Sweet & Maxwell, 1974.

Carapico, Sheila. "NGOs, INGOs, GO-NGOs and DO-NGOs—Making Sense of Non-Governmental Organizations." *Middle East Report.* #214 (2000). Online: http://www.merip.org/mer/mer214/214_carapico.html.

Census of Pakistan 1998. Government of Pakistan. Online: http://www.statpak.gov.pk/.

Chacour, Elias. *We belong to the land: the story of a Palestinian Israeli who lives for peace and reconciliation.* San Francisco: HarperSanFrancisco, 1990.

Chambers, Robert. *What Reality Counts? Putting the First Last.* London: ITDG Publishing, 1997.

Chaudhry, G.W. "Pakistan. Martial Law se Civil Hukumat Tak—Intiqal-e-Iqtidar ki Kahani." *Qaumi Digest.* Lahore, August 1990.

CIVICUS: World Alliance for Citizen Participation. Online: http://www.civicus.org/.

Civil Society and Governance—A Case Study of Jordan. Amman, Jordan: Al Urdun Al-Jadih Research Centre, 1999.

"Civil Society and Governance in Lebanon." *Lebanese Centre for Policy Studies.* Sussex: IDS, 1999.

Clayton, Andrew. *Governance, Democracy & Conditionality: What Role for NGOs?* Oxford: INTRAC, 1994.

Compilation of General Comments and General Recommendations Adopted by Human Rights Treaty Bodies. UN Doc HRI/GEN 1/Rev.1 at 38 (1994) paragraph 5.2.

The Constitution of the Islamic Republic of Pakistan. The Government of Pakistan Ministry of Law, Justice and Parliamentary Affairs (Law and Justice Division), 1994. Online: http://www.pakistani.org/pakistan/constitution/.

The Covenant of the Islamic Resistance Movement. 18 August 1988. Online: http://www.yale.edu/lawweb/avalon/mideast/hamas.htm.

Bibliography

Declaration on the Elimination of all Forms of Intolerance and Discrimination based on Religion and Belief, 1981. Online: http://www.unhchr.ch/html/menu3/b/d_intole.htm.

East Pakistan Assembly, Proceedings. Vol. XV, October 1, 1956.

"Egypt: Violations of Freedom of Religious Belief and Expression of the Christian Minority." In *Human Rights Watch. Middle East*. New York: Human Rights Watch, 1994.

El-Awaisi, Abd Al Fattah. *Umar's Assurance of Safety Aman to the People of Aelia (Islamic Jerusalem): A Critical Analytical Study of the Historical Sources*. Dundee: Al-Maktoum Institute Academic Press, 2005.

Electoral Law No 9 of 2005. Online: http://www.pogar.org/countries/countrylinksasp?cid=14&typ=5.

The Electoral Platform of Hamas. Online: http://lawofnations.blogspot.com/2006/01/hamas-party-platform.html.

Fottrell, Deirdes. "Ever Decreasing Circles: Affirmative Action and Special Measures under International Law." In *Minority and Group Rights in the New Millennium*, edited by Deirdes Fottrell, and Bill Bowring. The Hague: Martinus Nijhoff Publishers, 1999.

Fukuyama, Francis. *The End of History and the Last Man*. New York: The Free Press, 1992.

Gärde, Johan. *Religious FBOs and Secular NGOs*. NGO Management Program: American University of Beirut, Lebanon, 2001.

———. *NGO-Law and Civil Society in Syria*. Lebanon: Notre Dame University, 2005.

Global Civil Society At-a-Glance. Major Findings of the Johns Hopkins Comparative Nonprofit Sector Project. Baltimore, MD: Johns Hopkins Institute for Policy Studies. Without year. Online: http://www.jhu.edu/~cnp/pdf/glance.pdf.

Goldschmidt Jenny E., and Titia Loenen. "Religious Pluralism and Human Rights in Europe: Reflections for Future Research." In *Religious Pluralism and Human Rights in Europe: Where to Draw the Line?* edited by M. L. P. Loenen, and J. E. Goldschmidt. Antwerpen, Oxford: Inersentia, 2007.

"Guide: Christians in the Middle East." *BBC News*, December 15, 2005. Online: http://news.bbc.co.uk/2/hi/middle_east/4499668.stm.

Hairi, Abdul-Hadi. *Shi'ism and Constitutionalism in Iran*. Leiden: E. J. Brill, 1977.

Hammami, Rema, et al. *Civil Society and Governance in Palestine*. Sussex: IDS, 1999.

Heinze, Eric. "The Construction and Contingency of the Minority Concept." In *Minority and Group Rights in the New Millennium*, edited by Deirdes Fottrell, and Bill Bowring. The Hague: Martinus Nijhoff Publishers, 1999.

Hjärpe, Jan. "Some problems in the meeting between European and Islamic legal traditions. Examples, from the Human Rights discussion." In *Cultural Crossroads in Europe*, edited by Tuuli Forsgren, and Martin Peterson. Stockholm: Forskningsrådsnämnden, 1999.

———. *Profetens mantel: Den muslimska världen 2001–2006*. Stockholm: Leopard Förlag, 2007.

———. "Religious Affiliation as a Problem for Universal Ethics." In *Universal Ethics. Perspctives and Proposals from Scandinavian Scholars*, edited by Göran Bexell, and Dan Erik Andersson, 119–28. Dordrecht: Kluwer Law International, 2002.

———. "Revolution in Religion: From Medievalism to Modernity and Globalization." In *Globalization and Modernities—Experiences and Perspectives of Europe and Latin America*, edited by Göran Therborn. Stockholm: Forskningsrådsnämnden, 1999.

Bibliography

———. *Shari'a: gudomlig lag i en värld i förändring*. Stockholm: Norstedts, 2005.
Human Rights Monitor 2004. A report on the Religious Minorities in Pakistan. Lahore: National Commission for Justice & Peace, 2004.
Ibrahim, Saad Eddin. *The Copts of Egypt*. London: Minority Rights Group, 1994.
Issa, Anton. *Les Minorities Chretiennes de Palestine a travers les Siecles*. Jerusalem: Franciscan Printing Press, 1976.
Issues and Options for Improving Engagement Between the World Bank and Civil Society Organizations The World Bank, 2003. Online: http://siteresources.worldbank.org/CSO/Resources/CSPaper.pdf.
Jonasson, Ann-Kristin. *At the Command of God? On the Political Linkage of Islamist Parties*. Göteborg: Department of Political Science, Göteborg University, 2004.
Kandil, Amani. "Egypt." In *Global Civil Society —Dimensions of the Nonprofit Sector*, edited by Lester M. Salamon, et al., Baltimore: Johns Hopkins Centre for Civil Society Studies, 1999.
Kymlicka, Will. *Multicultural Citizenship: A Liberal Theory of Minority Rights*. Oxford: Clarendon Press, 1995.
Latham, Robert. *Non-Governmental Organisations and Civic Society in Syria. Report on the "Review of Association Law."* Workshop in Damascus organised by the Syrian Commission for Family Affairs (SCFA, March 22–23, 2005).
Lewis, Bernard. *The Multiple Identities of the Middle East*. New York: Schocken Books, 2001.
———. *The multiple identities of the Middle East*. London: Orion Publishing Company, 1999
MacLeod, Scott. "Vice Squad. The power of Saudi Arabia's morality police is being challenged, amid allegations of abuse and violence." *Time*. (August 6, 2007) 33–35.
Madigan, Daniel A. SJ. *A Common Word Between Us and You: Some initial reflections*. Online: http://www.acommonword.com/index.php?page=responses&item=51.
Making Services Work for Poor People. World Development Report 2004. Washington: World Bank and Oxford University Press, 2004.
Ma'os, Moshe, and Gabriel Sheffer. *Middle Eastern Minorities and Diasporas*. Brighton: Sussex Academic Press, 2002.
"Memorandum of Heads of Churches on Jerusalem." *Diocesan Bulletin of the Latin Patriarchate*. No. 20–25, volume 1, (January–February 1995).
Mishra, Naveen, and Sudhir Kumar Singh. *Status of Minorities in South Asia*. Delhi: Authorspress, 2002.
Modéer, Kjell-Åke. *Den svenska domarkulturen: Europeiska och nationella förebilder*. Lund: Corpus iuris, 1994.
———. "Optimal Legal Cultures? Modernity and Continuity in National and Global Legal Cultures." In *Globalization and Modernities—Experiences and Perspectives of Europe and Latin America*, edited by Göran Therborn. Stockholm: Forskningsrådsnämnden, 1999.
———. "Global and National Legal Cultures: Consciousness and Interaction of the National Legal Identity." In *Globalization and Its Impact—On Chinese and Swedish Society*, edited by Cecilia Lindquist. Stockholm: Forskningsrådsnämnden, 2000.
Moghal, Dominic, and Jennifer Jivan. *Religious minorities in Pakistan: struggle for identity*. Rawalpindi: Christian Study Centre, 1996.
Mughal, Aftab Alexander. *Aqliyaten, Insaaf aur Pakistan*. Catholic Naqeeb. Lahore.
Nadeem, Francis. *Yeh Des Hamara Hai*. Lahore

Bibliography

Nasr, Salim. *Arab Civil Society and Public Governance Reform.* Amman, Jordan: UNDP, 2005.
The Offences Against Property (Enforcement of Hudood) Ordinance. 1979. Online: http://www.sindhpolice.gov.pk/PDFs/offences_against_property_ordinance_1979.pdf.
The Offence of Qazf (Enforcement of Hadd) Ordinance. 1979. Online: http://www.pakistani.org/pakistan/legislation/zia_po_1979/ord8_1979.html.
The Offence of Zina (Enforcement Of Hudood) Ordinance. 1979. Online: http://www.pakistani.org/pakistan/legislation/zia_po_1979/ord7_1979.html.
Pakistan, Human Rights after Martial Law: Report of a Mission. Geneva: International Commission of Jurists, 1987.
The Pakistan Penal Code. Online: http://www.punjabpolice.gov.pk/user_files/File/pakistan_penal_code_xlv_of_1860.pdf.
Parshad, Joseph. "Pak-o-Hind Ki Tehreek-e-Azadi: Masihion aur Deegar Aqliaton Ka Kirdar," *Daily Pakistan.* (September 21, 1997).
Pitner, Julia. "NGOs' Dilemmas." *Middle East Report.* No. 214. (2000).
Political chaos takes its toll: A new poll says Palestinians are losing faith in their political leaders and want reconciliation between Hamas and Fatah. Fafo. July 18, 2007. Online: http://www.fafo.no/ais/middeast/opt/opinionpolls/180707palestinapresseeng.htm.
The Prohibition (Enforcement of Hadd) Order. 1979. Online: http://www.sindhpolice.gov.pk/PDFs/prohibition_enforcement_of_hadd_order_1979.pdf.
Promotion of Cooperation in the Area of Social Assistance Project. Progress Report (November 2005- July 2006). UNDP. Online: http://www.undp.org.tr/povRedDocuments/projectprogressreport.pdf.
Putnam, Robert. *Making Democracy Work: Civic Traditions in Modern Italy.* New Jersey: Princeton University Press, 1993.
Qanun-e-Shahadat Order. 1984. Online: http://www.sindhpolice.gov.pk/PDFs/qanun_e_shahadat_order_1984.pdf.
Raheb, Mitri. *I Am a Palestinian Christian.* Minneapolis: Fortress Press, 1995.
Rantisi, Audeh G. *Blessed are the Peacemakers: The Story of a Palestinian Christian.* Guildford: Eagle, 1990.
Rao, Ishtiaq. "Religious harmony essential for prosperity." *The Pakistan Observer.* (April 15, 2006).
Report of the Committee on Fundamental Rights of Citizens of Pakistan and on Matters Relating to Minorities, Karachi, 1953.
The Rights of Persons Belonging to Ethnic, Religious and Linguistic Minorities. (Capotorti Report) UN Doc E/CN. 4/Sub. 2/384/Rev. 1, New York, 1979.
Roy, Sara. "The Transformation of Islamic NGOs in Palestine." *Middle East Report* #214 (2000). Online: http://www.merip.org/mer/mer214/214_roy.html.
Sabella, Bernard. "Palestinian Christians: Historical Demographic Developments, Current Politics and Attitudes towards Church, Society and Human Rights." In *The Sabeel Survey on Palestinian Christians in the West Bank and Israel.* Jerusalem: Sabeel 2006.
Sabella, Bernard, et al. *On the Eve of the New Millennium. Christian Voices from the Holy Land.* London: The Palestinian General Delegation in the United Kingdom and the Office of Representation of the PLO to the Holy See, 1999.
Salamon, Lester, and Helmut K. Anheier. *In Search of the Nonprofit Sector 1: The Questions of Definitions.* Baltimore: Johns Hopkins Centre for Civil Society Studies, 1992.
———. *The Third World's Third Sector in Comparative Perspective.* Baltimore: Johns Hopkins Centre for Civil Society Studies, 1997.

Bibliography

Salamon, Lester M., et al. *Global Civil Society—Dimensions of the Nonprofit Sector.* Baltimore: Johns Hopkins Centre for Civil Society Studies, 1999.

———. *Social Origins of Civil Society: An Overview.* Baltimore: Johns Hopkins Centre for Civil Society Studies, 2000.

Salim, Ahmad. *Role of Minorities in Nation Building with Focus on Karachi.* Karachi: Church World Service—Pakistan/Afghanistan, 2006.

———. "Minorities of Pakistan: Struggle and Contribution." Unpublished paper.

———. *Religious Minorities in Pakistan: Are they Equal Citizens.* Islamabad: Frierich Naumann Foundation, 2006.

Salim, Ahmad, et al. *Violence, Memories and Peace-Building: A Citizen Report on Minorities in India and Pakistan.* Islamabad: South Asian Research & Resource Centre (SARRC), 2006.

Shahani, M. L. "Discrimination in Laws and its Impact on the Society." *Al-Mushir.* Vol. 46 (2004).

State of Human Rights in 2006. Lahore: Human Rights Commission of Pakistan, 2007.

Svedberg, Lars and Lars Trägårdh. *Sweden—A High Trust Society. A research Program.* Stockholm: Ersta Sköndal Högskola, 2007.

Tabbaa, Huda Sawaf. *Civil Society in Syria.* Washington: Civicus, 1999.

Thorberry, Patrick. *International Law and the Rights of Minorities.* Oxford: Claredon Press, 1991.

Universal Declaration of Human Rights, 1948. Online: http://www.un.org/Overview/rights.html.

Waqar, Ali. "Hate mongering worries minorities." *Daily Times.* (April 25, 2006).

World Christian Database. Online: http://www.worldchristiandatabase.org/wcd/.

The World Factbook. Washington, D.C.: Central Intelligence Agency, 2007.

Zia, K. R. "Tehreek-e-Pakistan men Masihion ka Kirdar." *Monthly Caritas*, (August 1997).

www.ingramcontent.com/pod-product-compliance
Lightning Source LLC
Chambersburg PA
CBHW050817160426
43192CB00010B/1798